# Why Suffer?

## How I Overcame Illness & Pain Naturally

··········

**Ann Wigmore**

HEALTHY LIVING PUBLICATIONS
SUMMERTOWN, TENNESSEE

© 2013 Ann Wigmore Foundation.

Cover and interior design: Scattaregia Design

Healthy Living Publications,
a division of Book Publishing Company
P.O. Box 99
Summertown, TN 38483
888-260-8458
www.bookpubco.com

ISBN 13: 978-1-57067-293-4

Printed in The United States of America

18  17  16  15  14  13          1  2  3  4  5  6  7  8  9

Library of Congress Cataloging-in-Publication Data available upon request.

Printed on recycled paper

Book Publishing Company is a member of Green Press Initiative. We chose to print this title on paper with 100% postconsumer recycled content, processed without chlorine, which saved the following natural resources:

- 13 trees
- 413 pounds of solid waste
- 6,170 gallons of water
- 1,138 pounds of greenhouse gases
- 6 million BTU of energy

For more information on Green Press Initiative, visit www.greenpressinitiative.org. Environmental impact estimates were made using the Environmental Defense Fund Paper Calculator. For more information visit www.papercalculator.org.

# Contents

# Foreword

I just came back from the town of Kruopiai, the remote village where Ann Wigmore grew up in Lithuania. I attended a memorial service there in the church where she was baptized. Afterwards, along with Viktoras Kulvinskas—who is also Lithuanian—and Brian Clement, director of *Hippocrates Health Institute*, and others, we erected a statue there in her honor in the bucolic town park. (Viktoras co-founded *Hippocrates* with Ann.) The townspeople were there in full regalia to help us celebrate Ann's life. It was a wonderfully festive and sublimely suitable event considering that this woman, whose influence ultimately spread around the world, started her life in this tiny town. I bought some wheatgrass seeds there that were locally grown along with a number of other seeds, herbs, and a few handmade woolens. Even in September, there was a cold bite to the air.

As the story goes, Ann was a sickly baby and her grandmother, a self-trained naturalist, helped and taught her how to use herbs and plants for her healing. But let the record be corrected, it was her midwife—not a biological relative but the woman who delivered Ann into the world—who served this role. Later in life, when Ann was injured in Boston and threatened with the amputation of both her legs, she recalled those natural skills and healed herself from gangrene. It wasn't long after that when Ann's gift and her life's mission as a healer began to blossom.

Although we called her Doctor Ann, she was not a medical doctor but a minister—a doctor of divinity. She was a simple woman who had no talent for science or research. Instead, she was driven by an inherent desire to help people.

She was indeed a minister, a servant of God, and, I believe, a prophet of health and healing. She was a soft-spoken woman who carried a simple but powerful message: "Why Suffer?" The body is designed to heal itself. Our modern lifestyles are causing our disease. Our fast food diet is corrupting our health. Our fears and emotions are mutating our cells. She beckoned us to eat simply, live simply, and simply follow the laws of nature.

I think what really got Ann motivated was that she came from a difficult, sickly, and impoverished childhood, yet she found malnutrition among affluent people living in the richest country in the world! She observed how we overcooked our food, overprocessed it, and polluted it with chemicals. Thus, she spent the rest of her life teaching people simple techniques for growing the purest food

The beautiful statue erected in memory of Ann Wigmore.

in the world. She showed us how to grow food from seed. It was indoor gardening, a return to nature available to those who had no land—even to those who lived in apartments in big cities, high above a cemented-over earth. She lived on those baby greens and used the life force in them to restore the health of her guests (she had no "patients") who came to her home. She also popularized the use of wheatgrass, which she used as herbal medicine. Outsiders made fun of her "grass," because in the 1960s it was the heyday of marijuana use. But Ann's grass represented hope, not dope.

On February 16, 1994, Ann Wigmore died of smoke inhalation from an electrical fire in her Boston home—the same home where thousands of lives were saved. The news of her passing spread far and wide, just as did her teachings. The planet may have lost her body that day, but the embodiment of her message carries on in the seeds she planted around the world. Her teachings continue to grow. To take responsibility for your food and control of your health, those are messages that will never die. Thank you and God bless you, Dr. Ann.

**–Steve Meyerowitz**

*Sproutman*®

# Preface

More than thirty years ago I began to develop my ideas on sprouting and indoor gardening to help myself. For years I had been plagued by bouts of colitis, arthritis, migraine, and a number of other health problems for which medical science had no solutions. I realized I had to change my lifestyle. I changed my diet and my mental attitude, and I began to exercise. A new pattern of life unfolded for me and prepared me for sharing and teaching my ideas. To accomplish my new goals I had to become more physically and mentally fit.

The change was remarkable. I came to have more energy than I ever remembered having. My weight returned to what it was in my early twenties, and my hair, which had begun to grey, returned to its normal brown color.

Following my personal successes on the diet and lifestyle, I established the Hippocrates Health Institute in order to reach out to people everywhere with the ideas and methods I used. Through careful observation of myself and others, I have come to several conclusions. We must give our bodies the rich nourishment from fresh vegetables, greens, and fruits; and sprouted seeds, beans and grains. When these foods are combined with proper rest and activity, and a healthy positive attitude, the body and will are strengthened and even the most serious health problems may be overcome.

At the Hippocrates Health Institute in Boston I have put these ideas and others to the test. Since its modest beginnings in 1963, thousands of people from all corners of the world have benefited from the two-week learn-by-doing program, which now includes a simple diet of fresh live foods, sauna and whirlpool baths, massage, daily exercise, counseling, and instruction for growing and preparing your own live foods at home. Today, the Institute has become a model preventive health facility.

The author gratefully acknowledges the typing and editing assistance of Marion Wickersham in preparing the manuscript of the tenth edition of this book. *Why Suffer?* was written as the result of a desire to explain fully why improving health and relieving pain and suffering is so deeply imbedded in my consciousness. The story begins with recollections of my early childhood growing up under the watchful eyes and care of my beloved grandmother, Maria, in a small war-torn village in Central Europe. As she was the local healer, Grandmother's skills were in great demand during those troubled times. She was responsible for repairing wounds and making important decisions in her capacity as a village elder, which helped insure our survival.

It was my grandmother who raised me and taught me the ways of natural healing. With her, there was no hopeless case. She was certain that any ailment could be relieved. Unerringly, she located in the nearby woods, fields, and swamps, the weeds, grasses, and herbs required for her work. Many mornings before daylight, I would journey with her into the fog, and while I could not distinguish in the gloom one plant from another, she would busily gather leaves, buds, grasses, and other plant materials. She was my inspiration and my teacher ever since I could toddle about, collecting the soiled bandages or tying the fragrant herbs into bundles for drying.

Grandmother did not believe, as did many people of those times, that physical ills were caused by a vengeful being—either devil or God—but that in some manner, the fault of all physical problems resulted from ignorance, neglect, or misdirected endeavors on the part of people themselves. It was not until I came to America that the truth of my grandmother's intuition—as to the man-made character of all illnesses—was made clear to me. I demonstrated in my own case and then in others that many ills could be attributed to excesses of certain nonessential nutrients, as well as a lack of essential ones such as vitamins, minerals, and trace elements, in the modern diet. Further investigations revealed to me the power of the emotions and beliefs in both causing and relieving physical ills. And so my grandmother's prophecy that I would learn to help individuals improve their lives and free themselves from problems, has shaped my life's work.

*Why Suffer?* ends with the founding of the Hippocrates Health Institute in Boston. A sequel to this story will detail my life and work during the past twenty-five years at the Institute. My encounters with hundreds of colorful personalities, and my lecture tours to more than thirty-five countries have had a tremendous impact on my life, and especially on my knowledge as a health educator.

There is no doubt a great hunger for balance in the lives of many people today. Thousands of people are turning to dietary change, exercise, and spiritual practices and studies in an attempt to find the balance and harmony they crave. In addition, individuals who can assist others in finding balance and harmony in their daily lives are increasing in number and importance. It is to these dedicated helpers, and to those who seek their balancing influence, that I dedicate *Why Suffer?*—in the hope that one day Grandmother's prophecy of a healthy, happy, and peaceful world, will also come true.

**Ann Wigmore**
January, 1985

# CHAPTER ONE

# Early Experiences

## THE FAR MEADOWS

In 1916, when I was approximately seven years old, I was able to help with the threshing of the rye and the chopping of the straw that went into the rough loaves of bread which made up our daily meals. The Great War had not as yet turned our village in Eastern Lithuania into a maelstrom of misery, but even then bands of marauders made frequent sorties through the valley spreading terror before them and leaving desolation in their wake. It was during one of these calamities that Hilda, the fourteen-year-old daughter of the widow who lived next door, and who took my grandmother's herd to the far meadows, disappeared. Some of the sheep and a few of the goats were later rounded up by the villagers. Other strays eventually made their way back to the barn, but there was no trace of the fair-haired girl. Later, the early assumption that she had been carried away by the raiders was proved correct.

Hilda and I had been close friends although I was much younger than she. I had accompanied her on three occasions to the far meadows, starting before daylight and returning after dark. But the journey was long, my legs were not yet strong enough and the trips had been too difficult for me. Even at the age of seven, I had no illusions as to what had happened to my friend. During previous raids, other women had been set upon and their mutilated bodies were found in some gully or among the great rocks that stood in many places.

It was my grandmother who after several days helped the boy Wolf, a neighbor, find the last trace of Hilda after she had passed through the swamp that fatal morning. The boy had been fond of my friend and there was fury in his eyes as he waved to us and started over the hill on the run, with his dog close at his heels. It was several hours later before he came into the brick oven room with clenched fingers containing the beads. I was in the far meadows with the herd and my grandmother told me later there were tears in his eyes as she confirmed that Hilda had worn the strand of blue beads that now lay broken on the table. He had found the place where Hilda had been forced upon a horse and her beads had dropped to the grass. There were the marks of nine horses and the trail led directly north, and Wolf had followed it for several miles until it crossed the sand dune region where the winds had effaced the tracks completely. Wolf's story confirmed the picture as the villagers had visualized it—Hilda had been kidnapped, probably murdered, and her body thrown into some distant crevice where it would never be found.

Each woman herder had been carefully warned to watch out for these marauders. They had been shown how to conceal their herds in the brambles and to hide until the raiders were gone. I could not figure out how Hilda had been caught. On one of my trips with her to the far meadows she had instantly caught the meaning of the sharp barks of her dog, and pushed the herd into the brambles. We had lain upon the ground, her hand on the dog's head to keep him quiet, until the horsemen had ridden away. But now she was gone and there was no herder for the remnants of my grandmother's flock. In such a place, Big Joseph, the overgrown son of the tanner of hides, could not be pressed into even temporary service. He meant well, but the vagaries of his mind made him careless. As my grandmother expressed it, "He's just absent-minded. The raiders would be upon him before he knew it. Yes, he is willing but he just won't do."

With that explanation her voice broke and there were tears in her eyes as she said, "Tomorrow, Annetta, you will take the herd to the far meadows. You will be my little sheepgirl. We have no dog now, but I know you will be careful."

And so, without fanfare, my status of a child of seven was changed to that of a full, useful member of the community, holding aloft the torch which had slipped so tragically from the inert hand of Hilda. In those days, the calendar meant little. Experience was what counted, as well as the ability to appreciate dangers and meet them with ingenuity. Yes, I was proud of the confidence placed in me and was up the following morning before my grandmother reached my bunk. It was still dark, with no sign of the coming dawn in the eastern sky, as I set out with the sheep and goats through the swamp towards the far pastures. This was the first of many hundreds of journeys I made during the years which followed.

Every morning before daylight, I would be awakened. My grandmother would sometimes have to dress me while I was still asleep on my feet and even feed me before I opened my eyes. Then I would start with the herd for the swamp. It was a difficult journey under ordinary conditions and in the half-light of the coming dawn, there was always a chance of some mishap on the slippery path. Perhaps it was the sureness of my faith in God's protection that made me certain I could live up to my grandmother's expectations.

My grandmother understood fully the risks, but in those days everyone was forced to undergo hardship. She, too, believed that the sheltering cloak of Heaven would afford me security. Each night, together, we would pray and offer our thanks for the blessings of that day and the blessings we both knew would await us on the morrow.

The far meadows lay west of the village, miles distant. To get there the herd must be guided along a narrow causeway through the quicksands. But day after day these dangers were overcome without accident.

During my first week of the routine that had been Hilda's, I guided the herd to the spring beneath the giant oak. There, with Big Joseph's help, I explored the place under the drooping branches of the weeping willow where there was a small opening in some brambles. This bare spot was a sort of natural hiding place into which the herd could be pushed in an emergency. Big Joseph lacked the alertness of Hilda and he failed to "feel" the approach of strangers in the distance. As I began to sense danger, however, I learned how two or three sharp commands would send the goats and sheep scampering off their feeding grounds and, in a few moments, they could be pushed easily into the hiding place by the spring.

Big Joseph was with me for about a month when work at the tannery forced him to say goodbye. I knew he did this with reluctance because he loved the woods and fields and I was sincerely sorry to see him go. It forced me to be alone from sunrise until after sunset. I missed the presence of human beings and particularly felt the absence from my grandmother. Nothing seemed to compensate for the loss of the kindly words of criticism and the smiles which lighted her tired eyes as I did something to please her. I even missed the groans and complaints of the sufferers who always filled the bunks in the room of the great brick oven.

But I soon discovered that I had been sent a substitute for human beings—the wild creatures that were everywhere. I found that each squirrel, each ground mouse, each bird, each snake, and each of the myriad of moving beings that make up the wonderful life of Nature had a distinct and pleasing personality. Perhaps it was because I was quiet, perhaps there were evidences, somehow intelligible to them, that I was extremely lonely, but something seemed to bring the little animals, unafraid, to my side.

I clearly recall my first visitor. It was a rabbit, a shy little thing with its right ear torn down the center, a memento perhaps of some miraculous escape from a hungry wolf during the previous winter. It appeared from the undergrowth close to the spring, just as I was studying the time by the shadows of the great oak against the ground. I knew it was close to midday, the position of the sun in the heavens being the only clock available for use. As I settled down on the grass and opened the basket of food, Mr. Rabbit (later I named him "Injured Ear") hopped closer. As I munched the sandwich of rye-straw bread and goat cheese, he jumped into my lap and, timidity gone, he nibbled at the tidbit I held in my hand.

His appearance and friendliness launched the series of long association which existed between me and the variety of other animals in that area. I believe it was the next day, at about the same time, that two squirrels, members of an extensive tribe dwelling among the leaves of the oak overhead, came down the rough bark in a series of short, hesitating moves. These curious spectators, whom I nicknamed "The Chatter Family," were soon at my side claiming their share of the slice of bread which I had placed on the grass for the rabbit.

And so started the routine that made me hostess at noonday feasts for this unusual collection of guests—from the white mouse which had belonged to a professor who had died, to Old Wisdom, the owl who could not fly, who lived in the hollow stump in the brambles.

Each day when the sun was directly overhead, I would leave my place in the meadows and slowly drive the herd to the protection of the willows. Then, ever watchful for signs of strangers in the neighborhood, I would sit down by the spring, my back against a protruding root of the great oak, and open my basket. To a casual observer I would have seemed all alone. Yet the moment the cloth was spread on the grass, my guests would come in silently. The squirrels, the birds, the mice, and other denizens of the surrounding thickets would find their accustomed places in the friendly little circle.

A family of porcupines, who lived in a hole in the rocky hillside to the west, would mingle at our dinner parties. From my meager store of food I had little to offer. Yet the rough bread of chopped straw and rye flour was popular with all those who came to our banquet under the great oak.

I discovered that creatures of the fields and forest could live peacefully together, and if not driven by fear or hunger, would not disturb each other or molest human beings.

As the days passed I became accustomed to this life cut off from human companionship, and I began to understand the strange and fascinating life about me. I learned firsthand something about health: that the wild animal, unhampered by civilized restrictions forced upon domesticated creatures, possesses energy and stamina even in times of want.

What a wonderful feast we enjoyed each day! Each creature was in a festive mood and there was no pushing or crowding. But as much as the visitors enjoyed these occasions, I, the hostess, was more pleased. Thus the long summer days were made livable and happy memories were piled up for a lonesome little girl whom circumstances had forced to take the responsibilities of an adult.

## MY BELOVED GRANDMOTHER

My grandmother, who was both my protector and benefactor, was an unassuming woman who possessed the touch of an angel. It was through her as Nature's handmaid that the miracles of healing which dumbfounded the inhabitants of the countryside were brought about. With her, there was no hopeless case.

I well remember on several occasions when children mutilated by savage dogs or wolves were brought to our farmhouse. My grandmother applied a poultice of some sweet-scented herb, which grew in profusion close to the barn of a nearby neighbor, to the bruised and broken flesh. The wound would usually heal rapidly without developing the raw, granulated edges so many of the wounded Russian soldiers exhibited when they appealed to my grandmother for help.

Early, I noticed another of her saintly characteristics: the more she accomplished in aiding the sick and restoring mutilated human bodies, the more humble she grew. She accepted no credit for her accomplishments. She merely thanked Our Father for the blessings which He so bountifully bestowed. In her I saw the kindliness and the unbounded faith of a believer. My own firm conviction that with His help nothing is impossible was rooted in my close association with this marvelous woman. Always, humbly, just before beginning her ministrations for some sufferer, afflicted with diphtheria or burning up with typhoid fever, she would place the responsibility of the outcome with God. As she had learned from long experience, so also I learned that with faith, mountains of obstacles and doubt vanished.

Coupled with this awareness, for me, was the realization of the close association of the physical being to the soul. I saw that when a human being was in harmony with God (some prefer to call it "Good") few problems of the physical body were unsolvable, no matter how strange and disturbing the symptoms might appear.

My grandmother did not believe, as some persons did, that physical troubles were caused by a revengeful higher being, but that in some manner the basis of all physical disorder was the result of ignorance, neglect, or misdirected endeavors on the part of human beings themselves.

She looked upon all abnormalities as the peculiar characteristics of the particular body involved. So on numerous occasions there would be smallpox, diphtheria, and typhoid sufferers in adjoining bunks of the great room and although my body was not yet strong, my grandmother would keep me in my bunk during the day, convinced that there was no danger. Her belief proved correct, for though the smallpox, diphtheria, and typhoid victims were all housed in bunks adjoining those unfortunates who were incapacitated by wounds, neither I nor any of the latter contracted these diseases.

It was not until I was here in the Western Hemisphere that the man-made character of some certain physical ailments was made plainer to me. Here I witnessed repeated demonstrations that many human diseases began when the body was weakened, was made susceptible to harmful organisms, by the lack of one or more nutrients required by the body's organs for healthy functioning.

As far back as I can recall, I was conscious of the comfort that only strong religious convictions can bring. This attitude was fastened by the almost universal feeling of utter physical helplessness on the part of the vast majority of the adults around me. They tried to find in divine guidance the reassurance needed in order to retain their sanity.

## A FROG'S WARNING

When I was about four, I was put to work outside in our garden. There was much to do. Shoes, of course, were unknown to my feet, and as the weather grew chilly, woolen cloths wrapped tightly served as their only covering. During that first summer I was sometimes carried to the nearby swamp to a spot where the freshets of the preceding spring had laid quantities of black mud along the banks. At a place where this wet and oozy mass was level with the surface of the sluggish stream, my grandmother would strip me to the skin and push me down into the warm, soft, yielding stickiness until only my head remained in view. Then she would step away and glance up and down the swamp. "If you hear the dogs barking," she would caution, "climb out. Don't wait to wash yourself. Hide under those bushes over there until things quiet down. I will come and get you." Then she would leave me and for hours my body would be drinking in the wonderful, soothing warmth from Mother Earth. My grandmother remarked, "The earth is filled with health-giving substances, and when the soil is wet and warm it benefits the human body in ways no other method can duplicate."

And so the lazy afternoons would slip away as I watched the fleecy clouds dodging between the treetops. I became interested in the insects which appeared to be standing on their long legs on the surface of the almost motionless areas of water near the bank, their legs ending in what seemed to be tiny flat shoes. One moment they would be motionless, and the next would go skidding along, propelled perhaps by a breeze.

I watched venturesome butterflies fall victim to the quick leap of a fish and I wondered at the solemnity of the frogs and mud turtles who eyed me, as an unfamiliar creature, from their cover under the distant bank. Occasionally, a water snake would appear, surveying my bodiless head with seeming distaste before gliding out of view under the naked roots of the willow down the stream.

As the summer days merged into the crisp fall, I found that my grandmother's predictions as to the health-giving properties of these mud baths were accurate. My body had rounded out, the indigestion which had plagued me seemed capable of being controlled and my constipation had vanished. (On several occasions, she helped elderly persons crippled with rheumatism to this same mud bath, buried them deeply in the soft, oozy mass, and, with head propped up by a handful of willow branches, they would sleep through long afternoons. Always, when they cleansed their bodies in the water by the great willow, they were delighted with the relief from pains and aches.)

It was Big Joseph who late one afternoon came out of the bushes across the stream and simulating surprise and horror at the sight of my head showing just above the mud cried, "Surely this is not the daughter of John the Baptist, sharing the same fate!" He unwrapped his great cloak, bundled my muddy body in it and carried me to my startled grandmother with, "Look at the mud turtle I found out there in the swamp."

I recall that in the second year of these mud baths I came close to a real adventure. I had been alone all afternoon, sleeping, when a big bullfrog with a deep bass voice landed plump on my face and let out an unearthly series of grunts which awakened me with a start. For a moment, I could not remember where I was, and then I realized that while I was asleep, the water had actually risen up to my ears. I struggled out of the mud and sat up. It was late in the afternoon and never before in the summer had I found the water so high. It must have risen six inches since I had been "planted" there soon after the noon meal. I climbed out hurriedly, donned my dress over mud and all, and fled home across the causeway over the quicksands.

My grandmother greeted me somewhat sternly because my clothing was literally covered with mud; she picked me up, she peeled off my dress, and washed me in the sheep trough by the barn. She listened intently, however, as I began to recite what had happened with the great frog. And then it came!

It began with a swishing sound to the north which gradually increased in volume until it resembled a roar, as the bank of water swept through the swamp, back of the barn. And then it was gone even more quickly than it had begun. But as Grandmother and I ran to the side of the garden and looked down at the swamp, the havoc created by the mad waters was everywhere.

Grass and branches and driftwood were in the trees, and the banks of leaves were swept away. But in a week, all signs of the devastation had disappeared and I was once more embedded in the mud bank.

My grandmother was deeply impressed by what had happened. She listened again and again to my story of how the bullfrog, jumping on my face, had awakened me just in time, how the suddenness of the feel of its cold body had aroused me so thoroughly that I had fled, mud and all. Her comment, as she nodded her head with deep understanding was, "I noticed the black clouds to the north after I got back from the swamp. I realized they were getting a heavy rain up there and I hoped it might spread to our gardens where the root vegetables are drying out. But I had no idea the storm was such a severe one. Luckily, Annetta, Mr. Bullfrog was sent to warn you. There are angels everywhere to aid in time of need."

## ASTONISHING VISITOR

Often, Grandmother would sit me under a great oak tree in the yard, and cover me with leaves. Leaving me with a thin cloth bag filled with crushed rye grains to nurse on, she did her chores inside the house. If I was asleep when night came, she would cover me with a woolen blanket and leave me for the night.

It was during one of those nocturnal leaf-covered sojourns under the great oak that I began my acquaintance with wild creatures. A new and thrilling experience! I had grown accustomed to the playfulness of puppies and kittens as they romped about me on the hay in the loft. But when I caught the odor and then saw the mother skunk slowly moving toward me in the dim moonlight, I was instantly alert. I watched her approach with the little ones tagging on behind. But I quickly realized the intruders meant no harm. So when she nosed my fingers I instinctively stroked her head just as I always stroked the puppies and the kittens. She seemed to like my touch and, sprawling lengthwise on the leaves, giving the little ones plenty of room, she contentedly nursed her brood. When the meal was over, she did not change her position as her kittens frolicked in the semi-gloom, diving into the leaf piles and frisking about on the grass. That started our friendship. Finally the mother skunk stretched, yawned like a cat, and curling up on the top of my small hand, went to sleep. I must have done the same. The next thing I remember was that dawn was breaking, my grandmother was kneeling on the leaves with my bowl of warm goat's milk and herbs, and the skunk family had disappeared.

As months turned into years, I grew stronger. Grandmother would sit me in the great oaken chair, "the throne," she called it, usually reserved for persons of prominence who were brought to our door from other villages for treatment. Thus ensconced, I would wash the bloody bandages, and later when I was able to move about, I would mop the slippery floor. Nothing was ever thrown away from the sickroom. Moss, dried and pounded into soft, fluffy balls, was used to staunch the flowing blood or wipe away the pus from an infected wound. But it was carefully cleansed after use and utilized again and again. In cases where the bandages must be wrapped tightly, the cloths were washed and allowed to dry in the sunshine. Where pus had thoroughly saturated the cloth, which was woven on the handloom in the adjoining "summer" part of the house, the woolen strip was washed in the stream back of the barn, rubbed with rye flour and allowed to bleach in the sun.

## A TRIBUTE TO FELLOW BEINGS

My first meals, and the meals I consumed for several years until I was strong enough to go outside and do my share of the community work, consisted of gruel made from crushed rye grain and diluted goat's milk. The rye would be threshed that morning on the barn floor, ground to powder between stones and mixed with the milk, still warm from the body of the goat. "The live grain will help you," my grandmother would say, "And so will the live milk. It is the only food a baby should have."

Grandmother never approved of cow's milk for anything but the feeding of calves. We did have a cow now and then when I was young, but later, during the hazardous prewar days, cows moved too slowly and were not as easily concealed in the brambles as were goats and sheep. These little animals seemed to catch the spirit of the hide-and-seek games that we were forced to play with the raiders, but the slow-moving cattle were soon all swept away from the village. Likewise, Grandmother never approved of milk of any kind for healthy adults. She looked upon all milk as medicine. It was her opinion that warm milk, taken from the goat standing beside my crib-bunk, was what saved my life. The cow's milk, which had been forced into my body as a tiny infant by a harassed mother trying to hastily fatten me up to endure a sea voyage, was one of the reasons for my difficulties. (Today, allergic reactions to cow's milk are not uncommon.) As my grandmother told a neighbor when I was about six years old, "The Almighty has mixed up Annetta's inside for some reason best known to Him. We must accept what has happened. She must always be careful what she eats."

Goats always played a distinct health role in our isolated lives. In fact, Grandmother believed that the goat was the closest of all animals to human beings. "The goat is clean," she used to say. "It is the daintiest eater and the most alert animal I know. A cow will eat most anything: dead hay, dead fish, and even the entrails of chickens. But not the goat! A goat, no matter how hungry, will shun anything that is soiled. If hay is contaminated in any manner, the goat will starve rather than eat it. The snobbish little creature always selects new leaves of shrubs and the tender inner bark of the trees. The cow stands calmly in the water in summer, chewing on the cud all day, while the goat is somewhere in the high places, balancing itself on some pinnacle about as big as your palm, where it can watch the happenings of the countryside. Give me a goat for milk to replenish the health of a stricken human body."

The manner in which my grandmother told of the richness of goat's milk was simple. She would draw a cup of water from the well and into the water she would let a drop of milk fall. The drop would sink slowly, almost intact. The drop which reached the bottom in the fastest time, was, in her mind, the richest.

So the goats and sheep were really members of our family. I heard later about another of the methods my grandmother used when I was first entrusted to her care, in her effort to build my strength. At sheep-shearing time she would have the matted wool taken from a sheep intact. She would wrap me in this, and for three days I would be a sort of mummy with just my head protruding from the fleece. This rather unusual treatment completely stopped my fits of coughing. She attributed special value to the oil of the wool, oil you could feel but could not see, though it did not make your hands greasy. This surface oil made it impossible for even a driving rain to reach the body of the sheep. "Something comes from the wool that helps sick human beings," she would say. She would often place it on an open sore or a wound, underneath the bandage.

But the use of milk as a medicine was something else again. The bread and milk poultice, made from stale rye-straw bread with the green mold showing and thick goat milk, was an ideal method for treating all surface disturbances of the body—boils, cuts, bruises, etc., from which the villagers suffered in and about their daily tasks. These poultices seemed to have extraordinary "pulling power" and my grandmother preferred this combination of bread and milk, when available, to the grasses and herbs she gathered in the fields, the woods, and the swamp.

I witnessed the clearing up of an arm injury—the flesh of which from the wrist to the shoulder was blue, bloated, and in a horrible condition. The man had been caught and held entangled in the barbed wire some soldiers had spread through the brambles at the sharp turn in the road a short distance below the village. For days the unfortunate man had lain there before someone, passing along the road, saw him, and stopped to lend assistance. He was brought into our house one morning just before I started for the far meadows with the herd. His condition was such that my grandmother asked me to remain and help with the bandaging. The two women carrying him were weeping in hopeless anguish, thinking the arm impossible to save. In those days, the loss of an arm was a calamity almost beyond comprehension. My grandmother washed the mutilated arm in warm water and laid upon it old pieces of rye-straw bread which she had soaked in new, warm milk from the goat which I had brought into the room. I remember well how that poor man moaned most of the night, but toward morning he fell asleep. When my grandmother wakened him, after I had left with the herd, the arm was better and the purplish-blue was turning to a dark pink. It took a full month to bring the torn flesh together and entirely banish the greenish cast of the sores. The muscles and ligaments had been injured permanently and while the arm could not be raised shoulder-high, it was still serviceable and could be used for ordinary farm work. Later, this man was one of the three villagers shot down in cold blood by soldiers, on suspicion of having had a part in the waylaying of a military raiding party some miles above the village. At the time that incident had occurred the man had been watching over his sick daughter in our house. All war is cruel, but sometimes its cruelties are beyond belief.

Grandmother used crushed grass frequently. She would grind the grass under the stones, place the pulp in freshly-drawn goat milk, and would pour it into gunshot or saber wounds before she would stitch the flesh together with an ordinary thread and needle. As I grew older, I often had to tie the pain-maddened sufferers in the heavy wooden chair so that no movement was possible during the sewing. Grandmother had no drugs to ease the pain.

All during the time I was an assistant to my grandmother the only liquids we used were warm water, crushed grass, and fresh goat's milk. But that combination seemed sufficient for all purposes. I do not remember a single instance where a sore or cut was not helped. Of course, in the matter of bullet wounds, where the bullet could not be extracted, or had irreparably damaged some vital organ, the sufferer would expire despite all the efforts we made.

## BLACKBERRY, CROW EXTRAORDINARY

In the early fall, after I had begun my duties as a herder, my spotted dog was killed by a pack of prowling wolves; but during the winter I acquired a new type of watchman, a friend who stayed with me for several years.

The winter had been most severe. Food was scarce, as snow had covered the ground for months and the wolf packs were lean and desperate. On this bleak and intensely cold morning as I walked beside the frozen stream in the swamp, I came upon a black, elongated object. I thought instantly that no life remained, but when I picked it up I sensed a flutter of the heart in the cold body. I thrust it inside my great cloak and pushed the herd toward the village on the run.

My grandmother was most interested in my find. She smoothed out the ruffled feathers, forced some warm goat's milk into the half-opened beak, and covered the body with a soft pillow. To me, her labor seemed useless, but in the morning when I was roused to take out the herd, she pointed to the pillow. And there, staring at me with its shiny black eyes, was one of the handsomest crows I had ever seen.

"Blackberry," as I called him, was my firm friend right from the start. Two months later when the weather was fairly mild, he rode in my great cloak to the far meadows and he seemed to enjoy the experience. That was the first of many trips he made with me during the rugged days of the new year. When the first signs of spring arrived, he perched upon my shoulder as we started out and when day broke in the east each morning, he would take flight, dodging through the trees and preceding just ahead of the slow-moving herd.

In an incredibly short time this sagacious bird changed from a mere friend into an actual protector. He divined the reason for my alertness and cooperated in my watch for strangers. Somehow, he recognized villagers and would ignore their presence, but let a stranger on foot or on horseback come into view in the distance, and he would swoop down from his high perch on the topmost pinnacle of the old oak with raucous squawks of warning.

At noontime, he would sit high above, quietly watching the countryside, occasionally dodging down to steal a tidbit from the tablecloth. He would accept no food from the hand of either my grandmother or myself. He preferred to snatch it and whisk away, or to stealthily pilfer something from the larder when no one was watching. Yes, Blackberry was just naturally a thief and many a trinket that had disappeared from the homes in the village I later found in his hiding place in the barn loft.

I learned so much from Blackberry. He never seemed in doubt for an instant and, guided by instinct, he made grave decisions in the flash of an eye, and those decisions always seemed correct. As my grandmother said, "Watch that bird carefully. The longer he lives the wiser he becomes. In his short existence he is allowed but one mistake, then everything is ended."

And the more I studied the actions of this feathered schemer and other instinct-guided creatures, the more I pondered over the infinite wisdom of Nature. Truly, I felt, "not a sparrow falls unnoticed in Heaven." Through it all I could feel the close connection that joins all human beings, animals, and plants. All are alive, all have their various duties to perform, and each group is dependent upon others for actual existence. Studying Nature's plan for this earth became the pattern for my everyday life. I would sit for hours watching the busy ants at work, always rebuilding, pushing ever forward toward some definite goal, never appearing discouraged. Plants, animals, insects, all life except human beings moved forward, never inert, never in doubt, pursuing their activities with a certitude that only the latter seemed to lack. That is why I never harm any living thing. My inner nature impels me to protect these little creatures at all times, no matter what the circumstances may be.

In the lush summer days there was no strife among the denizens of the meadows and woods. The field mice made no attempt to injure the baby birds which, unable to fly, would flutter helplessly in the tall grass. Everywhere about me were ample evidences that Nature was not cruel; in fact, Mother Nature was kind, loving, and considerate.

Thinking once more of Blackberry, he was indeed the wisest, most sagacious bird I have ever known. Also, he was friendly with the various dogs I pressed into service before I acquired Star.

### STAR FINDS A HOME

One well-remembered afternoon a skirmish took place along a distant road. It began with desultory bursts of echoing gunshots but gradually spread close to the house. Our windows were boarded up, so Grandmother and I watched through the small cracks along the lower sill after we had piled pillows and homemade rugs about the sufferers in the bunks. These were their only protection from chance bullets which might rip through the walls. Grandmother wanted me to seek safety in the shallow space below the house, there being no cellar, but I steadfastly refused to go until she also would seek refuge there.

We were much interested in a kindly young Russian named Ivan who was now trapped in the village by a body of enemy soldiers. When the machine gun bullets from the thickets below the public well began to smash the dishes on the shelves, grandmother pushed me through the trap door and I watched a tiny section of the battle through a hole, probably made by a rat, in the small flower bed along the wall of the house. There was little to see, so when the noise slackened and I heard my grandmother moving about the room, I climbed up beside her. The old man suffering from typhoid fever, in the bunk next to mine, was the only casualty. A machine gun bullet had torn through the top of his head. But the other patients were unharmed.

Now that quiet had apparently settled over the village, and despite my grandmother's objection, I slipped down the heavy shutter which closed the window over the brick oven, squeezed through, and dropped to the ground outside. I was worried about Ivan. I had paused long enough to reach back into the room for some bandages and a bowl of goat's milk. Almost at my feet lay a big Russian, the one who had always laughed so heartily. His face was almost unrecognizable and when I touched his arm, it was cold. At the woodpile, I tried to get the jacket off a cursing soldier whose bloody leg was nearly severed just above the ankle by the machine gun fire. He grabbed my bowl of goat's milk and drank it in spite of my protests, swearing loudly the while.

My grandmother now joined me, and when we saw the riddled barn we were glad that we had had foresight enough to drive the herd into the brambles beyond the swamp. At the well curb lay another shattered Russian, the one who had told me of his "red-haired little girl like you" in far off St. Petersburg, the little girl who would never see her father again. At the barn, near my horse's feed lot, was another wounded man. He had propped himself up against the rotting stump, his head weaving from side to side in agony. I pulled the barn door open, brought out some hay, and tried to make him comfortable.

It seemed incredible, but before we realized it, several of the villagers were in the yard. They helped Grandmother get the wounded into the main room of the house and the lifeless bodies were dragged out of sight behind the woodpile. I could not find

Ivan. Someone, I do not remember who, announced that there had been two prisoners taken away by the Germans, their hands tied to the saddles of the victors. It was some days later when two bodies, one the fair-haired, gentle Ivan, were discovered where they had been thrown after the firing squad had cut them down some distance away from the village.

The little dog who had accompanied Ivan from Russia, and of whom he had thought so much, had stayed with the lifeless form, though he was hungry and forlorn. It took men with pitchforks to push him away from the body so that it could be given to the quicksands in the swamp. The spirited mongrel, sensing its helplessness in a strange place without friends, was persuaded after a bit to accept my proffered affection. Soon we were inseparable and "Star," as I called him, became my lead dog on the journeys to the far meadows.

## HONEYCOMB RESCUES AN ENEMY

An incident during the war days illustrated how Fate sometimes returns good for evil in a most dramatic form. From our farmhouse, my grandmother and I had watched the ambushing by soldiers of a little band of enemy soldiers. It was late one afternoon and our attention was attracted to the scene by the loud outburst of gunfire from the brush-covered, abandoned clay pit just south of the village. There were five men, one an officer on a honey-colored Arabian horse that, frightened by the noise, reared and plunged about. This disorganized the troopers, who galloped off the road to the cover of a grove of nearby willows. But the badly wounded officer slipped into the dust as the yellowish horse streaked away with reins flying.

It was three months later when I saw that honey-colored horse again. It had come into the possession of Marcus, a cruel farmer, who had tried through continuous beatings to force it into the shafts of a hayrake. But the flying hoofs of the defiant animal quickly demolished the worn-out farm implement and Marcus was about to kill the beautiful creature when I appeared. A bargain was soon arranged. I purchased the now-quieted "Honeycomb," as I called him, by turning over my entire savings of years, which about equaled what his hide would have brought in the distant town.

Through the months which followed, I gradually won the confidence and affection of the mistreated creature although the scars on his hide would never disappear. It was really a splendid ending to many heart-breaking days, when on a wondrous morning I rode triumphantly into the village to prove to Big Joseph that my many tumbles and bruised arms and legs had been justified. But to the story:

It was some time later when great billows of smoke in the southern sky told of a possible catastrophe there. My grandmother was visiting ailing persons in that vicinity, so without a second thought I slipped onto Honeycomb's back, turned him around, and without saddle or bridle sped down the road toward the thickening cloud that was spreading over the blue sky.

As we passed the Marcus farm, Honeycomb suddenly left the road and before I could stop him, leaped the stone fence. There in the rye field, close to the stream, was a deep tragedy in the making. Marcus was stretched on the ground, a rattle-trap wagon with a broken wheel pinned against his chest as two half-wild horses thrashed about in their tangled harness. The farmer was a mass of bruises about the face and blood was pouring from a cut in his throat. As Honeycomb veered around the plunging horses, I jumped to the ground and managed to shift the weight of the wagon bed from the prostrated man. A moment more and I was able to stop the flow of blood and had dragged him to one side. I did not hear the approach of my grandmother who pressed in close beside me, or notice when the two men arrived who quieted the horses.

We carried Marcus to the house and made him comfortable, but the point of this incident, for me, lay in my grandmother's comments as we rode back to the village later. "Your quick action probably saved that man's life, Annetta, my child. He might have bled to death before I got there. It shows how God works. But for you, Marcus would have killed Honeycomb for his hide. Yet just now this same animal, alive and fleet of foot, brought you there just in time. It is a most worthwhile thought to have always with you—the most despised creature, ignored and seemingly unworthy of attention, may in the Almighty's scheme of things prove to be the link that spells the difference between success and failure, between life and death."

## TRUCE FOR A DAY

Blackberry was not friendly with Star. With them it was a case of an armed truce. They were jealous of each other and no matter how I tried, the animosity was always there. These two semi-wild guardians each tolerated the other merely because they knew I would permit no pitched battle.

On my daily journeys to and from the far meadows, Blackberry would lead the way far in advance, flying high to watch the countryside for army stragglers who might try to steal the herd from a little girl herder. Just in advance of the frisky goats would go my lead dog, Star, eyeing the thickets carefully for crouching wolves.

One day, when two of my sheep disappeared, Blackberry and Star seemed to understand my distraction, and buried the hatchet temporarily, working zealously together to help me. The pasture where the sheep grazed was a rugged piece of landscape broken by huge protruding rocks and deep gullies. As a rule, sheep feed together and very seldom become separated. But this particular morning, while my attention was on the chattering family of squirrels, two of the sheep vanished.

Although I searched all afternoon and into the night I discovered no sign of them. I went over a great portion of the pasture, inquiring of other herders if they had seen the missing pair, but to no avail. Most of the grazing sheep looked alike and I realized that if the two had mingled with another herd, picking out the missing pair might not be easy. The hardships of this battle-torn area made the other herders suspicious, too.

That night, because of the loss, I stayed there in the far meadows surrounded by my remaining sheep. Both Blackberry and Star seemed to sense my tension and its cause, and when daylight once more brightened the land, began scouring the country. Soon Blackberry was a speck in the blue heavens, as he circled slowly around like a hawk. You would almost have thought these two silent foes had caught something of my desperation. Naturally, I drove my sheep in many directions that morning seeking the lost ones, but my efforts were in vain. Star, his head hanging from fatigue, finally came back for a drink from the spring, and with tongue protruding, sank down under the willows.

The sun was not quite overhead when Blackberry returned. Even from afar, his loud squawks seemed highly excited. But I was overtired, and remained sitting dismally on the ground. However, what Blackberry wanted to impart was evidently caught by Star. He roused quickly from the shade, the hair along his back bristling, and fled through the underbrush toward the north. About ten minutes later the continuous, distant barking of the dog brought me to my feet and compelled me to push the tired sheep toward the sound. Blackberry was already circling over the agitated dog when I arrived at the pass where two rough men were guarding some thirty sheep. Star was on an adjacent hillock, a safe distance from their clubs, filling the air with his barks.

I realized that my sheep were in this herd. These two God-guided creatures, working together, had led me there. I talked with the men, who denied seeing my sheep. They did not know how well I knew my charges. I looked toward the grazing sheep and called, "Butter!, Still Water!" Immediately two sheep broke away from the herd and came toward me. The grizzled men could only gasp in amazement. These two thieves realized their danger, as the country was rough and the villagers were hardened. The men mumbled together and then apologized awkwardly, but I led my two sheep away and said nothing.

## MRS. CHATTER'S ACCIDENT

Before I was nine years old, my close association with the birds and other animals in the far meadows gained for me much appreciation of just how Nature, or God, has equipped these creatures to care for themselves in times of emergency and to know the proper method to obtain relief from accident and pain. Many times, when one of my noon banquet guests would refuse to eat and would sit quietly watching the other inhabitants of the wild place enjoy the tidbits, an examination of the body of the recalcitrant would usually reveal some half-healed cut or bruise. I began to comprehend, even at that early age, that Nature had definite laws.

It was during my first summer in the meadows that I had an opportunity to watch the healing power of ordinary mud upon the wild creatures, the same sticky mud which my grandmother used upon my body when I was a baby. As I mentioned, in the oak by the spring lived a whole colony of squirrels. One group, ruled over by a female grandmother, was the "Chatter Family." I had christened it thus because of the never-ending socializing its members kept up as they played hide-and-seek among the leaves overhead. The mother of a later generation, a pretty thing with reddish spots on her silky tail injured her leg in some manner. I had missed her for several days but gave little thought to her absence, until one afternoon when she dragged herself out of the tall reeds which lined the little stream. It was her left hind leg which had been injured. I noticed she had covered this limb with a dark clay which seemed to have hardened. I tried to get her to my side, proffering her a tidbit, but she only eyed me from a distance. When I moved toward her, she slid out of sight under the brambles, dragging the useless leg after her.

From the color of the "cast" on the little animal, I knew she had gone far down stream to where the sticky mud would cling to the reeds and bushes during the torrential rains of spring. The clever little creature had bypassed two small banks of less adhesive clay to reach this particular extremely sticky one!

It was probably a month before I saw Mrs. Chatter again. Once more she emerged from the thick grasses near the thorn bushes, but now the cast was gone. She was sleek and well-fed, showing perhaps that the other members of the family had not forgotten her during her difficulties. I knew she could not have climbed the tree to reach the supply of acorns which filled the hollow between the great branching limbs. With her reappearance, her shyness was gone. She came quickly to my lap for her share of the noon banquet and I had an opportunity to observe what wonders Nature, without the aid of human hands, could do. The leg seemed as well as ever, but there was a bump almost as thick as my finger (perhaps where a broken bone had not been perfectly aligned), but it seemed to cause no pain when I pressed it.

## A SKUNK SAVES MY LIFE

I first met Lady Albino, a pure white skunk, one Sunday morning when she followed me to church in a distant town. I was frightened because my head buzzed with the tales of the countryside, that an albino skunk is a mad animal which will attack anyone without cause and whose bite was as deadly as that of a poisonous snake. So a few months later, when Lady Albino came out of the willows one day at the spring and joined our family circle at lunch, I confess I was much disturbed. But the "lady" took her share of rye-straw bread in silence and seemed to arouse no antagonism among the various visitors—the owl who could not fly; Blackberry, my crow; Snow Flake, the white mouse; and the Chatter Family.

Thereafter, Lady Albino would appear regularly, take her place at the festive board, and after finishing would retire under the overhanging willows for a brief siesta before wandering back into the rough country to the west.

One afternoon in late fall I tarried by the spring, fascinated by the antics of the Chatter Family as they raced up and down the uneven bark of the old oak, when two outcasts appeared. Blackberry was nowhere in sight. The two seemed to rise up from the ground, so suddenly and silently did they appear. Both were unkempt and dirty, with their clothing in tatters. The larger one, with a scar across his left cheek, a flat nose, and small, piggish eyes, leered at me with a smile that was truly frightening. I did not understand their language very well, but I could make out from scattered words that they were planning to get rid of me, take my sheep, and drive them to someone in the north who would buy them without asking questions. The younger boy, who could not have been more than fifteen, was only doubtful about the best method of killing me. I knew they were ruthless, desperate, and that I was staring death in the face. The whole countryside had been ravished by the hangers-on of the two contending armies and piles of ashes and mutilated bodies in the undergrowth were all that remained of many farms. All these pictures flashed through my mind as I heard those two half-wild creatures whispering together. They would kill as surely as they would steal. This section was deserted, no help seemed in sight, and I realized forcibly that I must act before they moved. Yet young as I was, I knew I must not show alarm. So, ignoring the two who leaned against the tree trunk some fifteen feet away, I started to brush the flat earth near the spring. The next instant I leaped the small stream and plunged under the overhanging willows as fast as my short legs would carry me. I was headed for the thorn thickets beyond, where the narrow path would just enable someone as small as myself to squeeze through.

I heard the startled shouts behind, instantly followed by the smashing of the branches as the two crashed through the low growth after me. And then my foot slipped in the mud! As I went down their wolfish cries of triumph rang out. But their anticipated victory did not materialize. I heard the shriek of Lady Albino, who had been startled from her regular siesta, blended with the frustrated curses and cries as my two pursuers, blinded and suffocating, fought vainly against the ill-smelling mist which enveloped them.

Later, peeking cautiously from my hiding place in the thorn bushes, I saw that the ruffians were no longer interested in me. They had shed their clothing and with earth were trying to rub the obnoxious perfume from their hands and bodies. I was forgotten, my sheep were no longer attractive, and a bit later, the intruders were gone. That evening my grandmother made an extra tidbit for me to give to Lady Albino on the morrow—her reward for saving my life.

## STAR REPAYS A KINDNESS

I shall never forget the occasion when the treacherous sands almost received another body to add to those unknowns whom only eternity will again bring forth. And in the drama, Star repaid me in kind for my quick intervention at the time the frantic little dog was defending the body of his late master, the fair-haired Ivan, at the side of the road leading from town.

At that time the two patrol members might have run their pitchforks through the snarling animal had I not come between and sheltered him with my body. Even so, I received a gnashed arm from the bewildered little creature who was resolutely standing the final guard over the slain man in the tangled grass. Thus came about the advent of Star into our community, and early next morning, almost before daylight, when I marshaled him with the herd preparatory to the dangerous trip through the swamp to the pastures in the far meadows, his sense of familiarity as to what I might expect of him suggested that somewhere in his brief career, he had worked with either goats or sheep in far-away Russia.

My grandmother liked the little animal from the start and even the first morning, before she closed the barn door after us, slipped him a tidbit from the breakfast table. So in the days and weeks that followed, Star proved a useful teammate for a nine-year-old girl who had to face the rugged existence of that war-torn countryside alone. He helped conceal the herd from groups of marauders from both armies, and in the winter aided in fending off members of lean wolf bands which, half-starved, stalked the isolated herds and pulled down any straggler which momentarily got separated from the main drove. Slow-moving sheep were particular victims of these assaults, while the agile goats, with their sharp horns, could hold the snarling, emaciated creatures at bay until Star's long fangs sent them scuttling under the thickets.

It was a quiet evening in late summer. The sun had set and the path along the hillock above the sluggish stream was thick with dust, which probably accounted for the presence of the large black snake trying, possibly, to get the last of the warmth which the deep, loose earth contained. Star, who usually proudly led the way, had slipped back to my side where I was carrying a little newborn lambkin in my apron. Anyway, the quietness of the scene was suddenly broken as two goats who were leading the silent procession spied the snake and whirled back upon their fellows. This panicked the solicitous mother, "Ida," about the safety of her offspring. She bumped into me, causing my apron to fly open. The little lamb fell to the path and I tumbled down the slanting bank into the waist-high water.

My long experience with this section of the swamp impressed me with my danger. I had landed on quicksand where the bodies of many an unknown soldier had disappeared during the savage fighting of the roving guerrilla bands, when the villagers had to hide all evidence in order to prevent the sacking of the community. I knew, as the sand began to pull me into its maw, that I had but few minutes to live. I could not clamber up the steep bank and every moment brought me closer to the end. Star was leaning far over the edge, wanting to help. When I cried, "Get Grandmother!" he understood what he was to do and was off instantly. I heard his frantic barking grow fainter and fainter as he sped toward the village. I was up to my chin in the murky waters when the strong arms of Big Joseph reached down from the path and slowly freed me from the nightmare, answering my prayer. I slumped into my grandmother's arms. Star had more than evened accounts, and that night he slept on my feet in the bunk while my grandmother fed me herb gruels.

## LONG HAIR, A GOAT WITH A MIND OF HER OWN

Many times, I saw in all its details how Nature cares for the wild creatures. This time it was an accident, perhaps the bite of a venomous snake or insect. The victim was a goat named "Long Hair," and Grandmother was of the opinion that had the little animal been permitted to roam wild in the meadows and select its own food instead of subsisting on the dried hay in the barn through the winter months, the bite of the snake or insect would have had an almost un-noticeable effect. I do not know when or just where it happened, but I noticed on the way towards the swamp in the dimming light one evening that Long Hair was limping badly. By the time we arrived at the barn one of her front legs had swollen to twice its natural size and the suffering animal could hardly stir.

While I held the little goat, Grandmother applied poultices of herbs to the injured limb. But as we could discover no wound indicating the spot where the poison had entered, we wrapped up the entire leg and fastened the two front legs together to keep the squirming animal from ridding herself of the bandages. Next morning, bandages and all, Long Hair refused to stay in the stable. And finally relenting, I let her join the herd for a few moments and then tied her to the thick vine beside the woodpile. When I started with the other animals toward the swamp, Long Hair set up such a racket from this vantage point that my grandmother came out of the house, removed the bandages and set her free. Even in this brief period, the swellings had begun to subside, and with her bringing up the rear we trudged slowly toward the far meadows. When we came to the mudbank which lined the stream beyond the quicksands, Long Hair deliberately slid down the slope, sinking up to her belly in the soft muck. She straightened herself, looked up at the barking Star with a half-pitying appearance and almost smiled with satisfaction.

This posed a difficulty. Long Hair refused to budge from the stream and I could not dislodge her with my long stick. Of course, I could turn the herd about and go back for aid in the village or I could continue my journey and leave her there. She was one of my grandmother's best milkers and the country was filled with wandering marauders. I sent Star down the bank to push her along to where the path dipped almost to the level of the stream. But the little goat had other ideas. Usually patient and obedient to Star, her sharp horns kept the barking dog at a distance, until I gave up the battle and sent him up on the path once more and our journey continued toward the distant meadows without her.

When we returned, after the fall of darkness, Long Hair was still in the mud, chewing industriously on the end of a piece of driftwood, but the grass along the overhanging bank had not been touched. This time, when Star splashed into the stream, Long Hair roused herself, climbed the steep side and loped off toward the village as though the still swollen leg gave her little pain or inconvenience.

The next day, the same procedure repeated itself, although I tried again to keep her on the path and again we went on without her. But on the third morning Nature seemed to have the situation in hand because Long Hair limped to the far meadows with us. Within two weeks there was no sign of swelling.

My grandmother viewed the outcome as entirely to be expected. "Our goats receive mostly just the nourishment God intended them to have," was her comment. "Yet we must feed them a great deal of dry grass in the winter-time. Fortunately, the pastures in the spring, summer, and fall do much to fortify their bodies for the ordeal of the snow and sleet. You can hardly expect an animal herded into the barn and fed bleached hay to be able to heal itself easily. It needs the green of the grass which has vanished in the cured hay. Some day we'll know what happens to the green which is so plentiful when the vegetation is growing and which disappears so quickly when it has been severed from the roots. You must study, Annetta. You must learn what I have been unable to learn. This small village is my world, these people I love, but I realize that while we may have wisdom, we do not have what the books teach."

## STAR DISAPPEARS

The health-giving advantages of fasting, as I had observed them among my visitors at the spring in the far meadows, were impressed upon me more strongly when Star came down with an illness. The little animal evidently felt some abnormalities arising in his body because he found a "substitute" to take his place with the herd, a nondescript, curly-haired creature we knew as "Shaggy" and with whom he had battled regularly until this time.

One evening, Star had all the visible symptoms of "the mopes," as my grandmother called them: a hot nose, eyes full of discharge, and a weakness in his legs so great he could hardly stand. Before my grandmother could help him with an herbal brew he had slunk away into the darkness and disappeared.

"He's hidden under the woodpile or deep in the brush," was her comment. "I've noticed that trait in animals. When they are really sick, they seek solitude, away from tempting food of all kinds and even from water. And this resting of their digestive processes gives Mother Nature an opportunity to muster her healing powers with nothing to interfere with her work. Human beings do not always have that much sense. The family hovers about the ailing one, plies wine, milk, and other food 'to give strength' and in my opinion sometimes causes the death of many unfortunates whom they love and only seek to help. When you seemed to be dying, Annetta, I kept even warm goat's milk from you. The little two-year-old daughter of the Gustaitis family was not nearly as ill as you—her throat was partially open—but whose aunt forced thick soups into her weakened body despite my protests, passed on within two days. You, on the other hand, who seemed doomed for an early death from birth, came through stronger than you had ever been before."

It was two weeks later that Star came out from under the woodpile and dragged his thin body to the sheep trough near the well. He could hardly move and could barely lap the goat's milk my grandmother brought from the barn. But the distemper was gone, and his strength came back rapidly. The long fast had done its effective work.

**NIGHT HAPPENING**

It was 1915, the second year of the Great War. Our countryside had become a no-man's land for small bodies of depredators from both the contending armies. Their excesses seemed to know no limit and their cruelties left scars from which the villagers never recovered. Sudden death became a mere incident in our lives. While we were accustomed to the harshness of Nature, we now had to add these inhumanities of man to our outraged knowledge. But while the villagers were cowed, brow-beaten, and reduced to servitude by these marauders, on occasions the latent spirit of retaliation would rise in a sudden white-hot flare. It was after one such burst that the full potential of the quicksands in the swamp was violently brought home to me.

The occasion was late one night, just after I had bedded down the herd and was starting toward home. A group of three soldiers had been carousing in one of the houses down the road, and on leaving had dragged the young wife of the farmer towards the horses to carry her away. This had been the spark which spread fury among the other villagers, and they fell upon the terrified kidnappers with clubs, beating them into the dust and trampling them with their heavy boots. It was all over in an instant, but the entire village was involved and my grandmother, greatly alarmed, took charge at once. All up and down the countryside piles of ashes marked the places where farmhouses had stood and unmarked piles of dirt were the silent evidence of the vengeance of the enraged military.

Quickly the bodies of the slain were dragged into the brambles and covered with leaves. Women with branches smoothed out the rumpled soil and banished all signs of the struggle. The three horses were unsaddled and the equipment hidden under piles of hay while the animals were taken into the rocky country to the north and set free by the boys and girls. I was just a spectator, peeking through the cracks between the boards that covered the window facing the north. Later a group of silent men moved the two wheeled, straw-covered cart past our barn and into the swamp beyond. I did not need to be there to know what was happening. The bodies, saddles, and bridles were given to the quicksands and all evidence of the trouble had vanished by the time I pushed my herd over the causeway just before dawn on the following morning. And as time passed, the silent journey to the sands was repeated whenever the body of a soldier would be found along the road. Grandmother said, "Only the Almighty knows best. Our lips are closed and the swamp holds the secrets in its bosom."

## BIG JOSEPH AND THE BIRDS

It was slow-witted Big Joseph who showed me a method of attracting birds. His whistle was unlike anything I had ever heard. It did not resemble any call of the feathered tribe, yet when he placed his fingers to his lips and sounded the shrill notes, it would be instantly followed by a flutter of wings and in a few moments this giant of a man would become a motionless statue covered with winged messengers struggling to find a place on his enormous frame. For some reason, the jays and the blackbirds, usually natural foes, would forget their differences temporarily as they balanced themselves, side by side, on his outstretched arms.

My grandmother loved to tell how, one afternoon on the village street, she had seen Big Joseph seated silently on a stump with his huge body literally covered with dozens of birds of various kinds. I learned from Big Joseph the little chirp-squeak which sent all of our feathered friends quickly into hiding. Does this indicate that birds have a sort of universal language which each species understands? He taught me also a singsong sort of wail that could put them all in the air at once, and as time went by I could follow the meaning of the chirpings high up among the leaves almost as well as I understood the tongue of my grandmother.

## VICTORIA AND THE WOLF

As I look back upon that life, I realize fully that I was a sort of wild thing myself. I had never received any schooling except what was taught in this great school which Mother Nature conducts continuously for all who wish to tarry and learn, and by my wise grandmother. In the summertime, wolves posed no threat. Star, now almost an untamed creature of the open spaces, while posting himself between the watchful packs and the herd, made no effort to drive them away during the warm weather.

One of the strangest happenings which clings in my memory concerns "Victoria," a little white she-goat, and the fascination a certain tan wolf with a brownish ruffle of hair about his neck had for her. Victoria would stand poised on a tiny pinnacle of rock, hardly as big as your fist, and twirl and dance every time she would see him watching from a neighboring hillock. But this seeming mutual attachment ended in tragedy the following winter. The heavy snows had been too much for the wolves, and half-famished, they roved in packs seeking food. It happened when the snow had drifted high, and hungry marauders, led by the tan wolf with the hair ruffle about its neck, broke into our barn. The noise aroused us, but when we reached the scene of the trouble, Honeycomb the horse had frightened away the intruders. But little Victoria lay dead, with her long, saber-like horns piercing the heart of her summer admirer.

## THE STORY OF CRINGY

My knowledge of the meaning of the different sounds made by animals probably saved the life of the farmer Marcus a second time. A rockslide had pinned him down in an isolated little gully back of the rough region to the west. I knew the usual howl of "Cringy," as my grandmother called his slinking, ill-treated little dog, but this time there was something strange in the whimpering wail that sounded to me like a plea for help. The remembrance of that little, plaintive cry haunted me all day. It came to my mind repeatedly as I drove the herd back past the spring. I wondered what Marcus could be doing in that part of the far meadows which was almost devoid of grass or young growth for his goats. Arriving home, I spoke to grandmother about it and learned to my surprise that Marcus had not been seen for several days. His house was deserted and neighbors had turned his bellowing, thirsty animals out into the fields.

As a result of my story of having heard Cringy's mournful whine that morning in the rough country back of the far meadows, concerned neighbors immediately turned their search to that region. Marcus was found dying of thirst within five feet of a cool pool of water. His mistreated little dog had not deserted him. It had remained on the high bank overlooking the little gully, sending a plaintive cry for help into the air.

Fate is often unkind. I cannot leave this story about the faithful dog without telling of the event which happened hardly two weeks later. A neighbor had gone to the Marcus farm for a sack of rye, but seeing Marcus needed a cow badly, had made a deal for more grain. Marcus prepared to hitch up his wagon to deliver the seed. As he struggled with a shying horse, the heavy wagon was accidently backed over little Cringy, who had been tied by his master to the spokes of the rear wheel. Yes, sometimes Fate is hard to understand.

## THE WOUNDED

When the hazards and hardships of war conditions settled over the village and surrounding countryside, I found that my duties were greatly enlarged. There was much more to do than merely look after the herd during the day. That was but a part of the demands upon my time. In the evening, after I had bedded the herd in the barn, I would slip into the house. Pausing at the door I would try to distinguish in the gloom the occupants of the bunks extending along the side walls. Generally I could pick out the new arrivals and the piles of litter on the floor were fairly accurate indicators of the extent of my grandmother's efforts since early morning. Usually there were two or three groaning men along the north side where the wounded soldiers were housed. Few sounds came from the opposite wall, generally given over to disease-stricken villagers. Upon my arrival I would be asked to hold some shattered arm or leg while the temporary bandage was changed to a more permanent one for the night.

Occasionally, according to the fortunes of the borderland war, we would have an army surgeon present, either a Russian or a German. These highly educated doctors, without exception, seemed to venerate the natural skill of my grandmother. One German surgeon I remember well. His chest was covered with decorations, which he wore despite the quips of two fellow surgeons, who left him in my grandmother's care because of his crushed toes. This fierce-looking giant with the bristling mustache was one of the loudest complainers about pain that had ever stayed in that brick oven room. He moaned continuously as we worked over the crushed toes with warm water and herbs, Grandmother disdaining to use the wax package of salve on the window sill for which he kept reaching. We made him comfortable in the big chair by the window, and twice during the night Grandmother changed the bandages. By morning, when the leaves were unwrapped from about the toes, the bluish-purple lines had disappeared and the man expressed his grateful-ness in deep gutturals I did not understand. For a week we had him as our star guest and when the two brother surgeons returned they could hardly believe what they saw. They patted my grandmother on the shoulder, drank a toast to her with well water, and when they helped their limping fellow surgeon to his horse, he leaned over and kissed her as "Meine Mutter!"

Our experiences were frightful sometimes. I remember hold-ing the arm of a pain-racked young boy in Russian uniform whose hand had been crushed under the wheel of a heavy wagon. I can still hear his screams of despair as grandmother cut off the flat-tened and dead fingers. Another time, we had to put the intestines of a soldier back into his body when he had been slashed by a saber. We cleaned the exposed internal organs as well as we could but my grandmother told me sorrowfully that he would be dead by morning. And her prediction was correct.

During these trying times, my grandmother seemed under divine protection. She was the uncrowned leader of the village. The farmer with the white beard who had been the patriarch of the community had been murdered by a band of marauders. I do not believe anyone suggested to my grandmother that she take command. It just seemed to the villagers that the logical thing to do was to give her the final say when decisions were to be made. Even when the soldiers were billeted in the houses, she was permit-ted to come and go about as she pleased.

One evening, a great, hulking German officer fell from his horse at our door, and pulling his tunic aside exposed a wound which extended across his whole abdomen. It was evidently an old wound which had opened up and it was oozing pus. He was covered with some strong-smelling oil which he cursed as being of little use.

My grandmother did not hesitate a moment. Motioning to me, we pulled him into the house. He was too heavy to get into the bunk and seemed to have passed out. I heated the water and Grandmother left me to go into the swamp for fresh herbs. When she returned the wounded man was conscious and as she cleansed the wound he confided the story of his family in far-away Frankfurt-on-Main and his profound longing for peace. All night the man sipped the brew and I changed the bandages on his abdomen every time they became cold. The treatment was effective and when he finally rode away with his two orderlies who had arrived the following morning, there were tears in his eyes as he bade us goodbye.

Two years after the war ended, when I was preparing to go to the Western Hemisphere, a long letter came from the wife of this officer. She thanked my grandmother for the care she had given her husband and enclosed her wedding ring. "My husband is now no more," she wrote, "but you did save him for the little anniversary gathering of our wedding before he was sent into France, where he was killed. I am penniless now but I hope this gift may, in a measure, show how much I personally owe to you and your little girl."

## ESCAPE

Many times during the war-torn days in that little isolated village I saw how effective were the herbs that were Nature's medicines. Grandmother called herbs and grasses "medicines," made by the sun in Nature's blue-domed workshop.

While I grew up from babyhood appreciating the help herbs could render in the sickroom, it was our dreadful experience in the root cellar that made me understand what ordinary grass could do for the human body.

I shall never forget the morning that Big Joseph came breathlessly to the far meadows to warn me to hide my herd securely in the rocky country back of the spring. Several other villagers were also pushing their sheep and goats into this uncertain terrain, which was dotted with tiny valleys filled with tall grass. A battle was brewing and Grandmother wanted me home with her when it began. So I left Star with the herd and worked my way with Big

Joseph back through the brush into the village. And just in time. A large band of soldiers swept down from the northeast, took possession of the houses, drove the inhabitants from their homes, and began stringing barbed wire between the trees.

But Grandmother was equal to the emergency. She herded us into an abandoned root cellar in the destroyed orchard, a cellar which two years before had sheltered a Russian machine gun nest. Eventually this gun emplacement had been destroyed by the German artillery, leaving most of the fruit trees lifeless, their bare branches reaching to the heavens as if beseeching help. There must have been twenty of us crowded into that muddy hole. Only the small children could stand upright and I marshaled these to one side where leaves and branches made a sort of carpet over the mire. And so we all crouched in terror while the machine guns rattled above and the ground was made to tremble now and then by a distant explosion.

Strange as it may seem, I do not know how many days we were held prisoners in that black pit of misery. I do remember that on the morning of the second day, our food ran out and many children whimpered miserably. Several villagers were already sick from drinking the muddy water at the lower end of the hole.

That night there was a driving rain with rolling thunder replacing the bursting shells. But this storm increased our discomfort. Little streamlets trickled in from outside and the clothing of all was soon water-soaked. But my grandmother never faltered. In her steady voice she kept reassuring the apprehensive. Over and over she told them that everything would soon right itself.

Next night, when the rain had slackened a bit and the outside was black and silent, she pushed up the wooden cover of the root cellar and disappeared. We waited tensely for the expected rattle of shots, but none came. It seemed hours before two low knocks sounded on the wooden planking above our heads, and when Big Joseph placed his great hands against the cover and lifted it, Grandmother slid down to join us. She had found several handfuls of dried vegetables which she had tied in her apron. She handed me a large bunch of freshly gathered grass. I shall never forget how wonderful it tasted as I shared it with the hungry little tots all about me.

The following night, my grandmother vanished again, and although the rain continued, she brought in more food and additional quantities of grass. But by morning tragedy had struck. An old man pulled the limp bodies of a little girl and her mother to the front of the cellar. They were beyond help, drowned by the muddy water which had risen slowly, so that the rear of the hole was flooded almost to the roof. This calamity was a stunning blow for all of us. We knew that this cellar was in a cup-like formation and in the spring sometimes flooded. We shuddered as the thunder rolled across the dark skies.

I can see my grandmother now—outlined against the lighter gray of the half-raised roof. She spoke in a calm voice everyone could hear and outlined the bleak facts of the situation. Then she made the decision that might cost some of us our lives. In a few minutes, Big Joseph would push back the cover as quietly as possible. Then we were all to crawl single file up the slanting bank into the heavy, rain-soaked darkness right before dawn. It would be the job of the men to carry the children and the younger women to help the aged. But it was each one for himself and herself. As Grandmother put it, "Make no noise. Run as you have never run before. Scatter in all directions. Let us know that God will allow some of us to reach safety." She stopped speaking and taking me by the hand helped me through the opening that Big Joseph was enlarging.

Thoroughly frightened, I knew that I would get through to the bushes that grew along the broken fence near the path that ran toward the home of Speechless Anna. And somehow I felt certain that my grandmother also would survive. As she had said, it was better to die like human beings in the open air than be drowned or trapped in that hole.

All I remembered is clutching my grandmother as we plunged through the mud toward the lane. In the darkness I stumbled over a body and would have fallen but for a grip on my hand. The next moment we had freed ourselves from the mud and were speeding across the wet grass, the rain pelting down. Everything was quiet except our slopping footsteps, and then from the distance came flashes of yellow light. Bullets whistled through the orchard. They buried themselves in the tree trunks with resounding thumps. I heard the despairing wail from Himma, the young mother who lived in the little house by the three oaks. She must have been the first one struck by the cross fire, but her cry was almost instantly followed by shrieks of pain and hopelessness from other points in the orchard.

We reached the brambles and burst into the thick foliage. My grandmother dropped into the mud, pulling me low and pressing against the soggy earth. Here we waited for some time before moving. We heard the moans and cries from back among the trees but could offer no help. Then the bullets ceased and as daylight was beginning to show in the east we crept into the lane, slopping through the mud and into the thickets beyond. Not a word was said; we just pressed on until we reached the uninhabited country to the north of the swamp where we felt we were safe.

All that day we lay under the protection of an overhanging bank. It was near sunset when the rain ceased and the rays of the late afternoon made the drops on the leaves glisten and sparkle like a myriad of jewels. Three other villagers joined us, but could give us no word as to how many others had survived. We worked our way to the "haunted" house hear the ledge of rock and prepared to hide until morning. We had no candles, and of course would not have lit any if we had had them. Our clothing was still damp, but I managed to sleep. It was near midnight when I found myself on my feet in alarm as a great pounding sounded on the door. But the shouts of Big Joseph were most reassuring. He brought glorious news: the war was over and we could now return to the village without fear. It was certainly a memorable night for me in many, many ways. I found that my grandmother had been wounded in the side the first night in the root cellar, but she had kept her secret well. I did not like the looks of the bluish-purple swelling where the bullet had gone through, but she only waved her troubles aside. While the other villagers were celebrating and talking exuberantly, she pulled me out of the house to a place on the broken well curb.

CHAPTER TWO

# Toward the New Goal

## A PROMISE

"Annetta," she had said. "This is the end of the awful strife, but it is a new beginning for you. Your star is across the distant ocean, in the land where your parents live in comfort. I have raised you for the purpose of helping others when I am gone, which may be closer than you realize. We have a hard time ahead and it may take years of slaving to earn the money for the ticket." "No, no," she said with emphasis as I sought to stop her, "I must remain here. My daughter and the two babies need me now that the father of the family is gone. But you know how to help the sick. Up to now you have been my able assistant. Across the ocean you must be my emissary of helpfulness, where it is needed. We will not speak about this again. This is a joyful night—peace throughout the world—and I want you to seal my happiness for all time to come with a promise that you will do as I ask."

And so, in the yard of that haunted house, I gave her my word. Receiving my pledge, she kissed both my eyes, as tears streamed down our faces.

## UNWANTED

Of course, the incidents of my babyhood happened without my remembrance. I had grown up as a part of my grandmother's household, never realizing the hardships she endured on my behalf. It was not until now that the full details surrounding my babyhood were laid before me by friends and neighbors.

I was born in Cropos, a small, isolated village in Lithuania, nestled in a valley that was constantly ravaged by armed bands of marauders. Before my birth, my parents had planned to leave the region for the brighter horizons across the Atlantic, and my arrival at an inopportune period, thin and sickly, transformed me into an object of dismay and even hatred. The war clouds between

Germany and the rest of Europe were already gathering and the horrifying possibilities of such an impending catastrophe terrified my father.

My grandmother intervened. While she was uncertain as to her ability to help me through the crisis of babyhood, she declared her willingness to assume all responsibility for me. This offer permitted my parents to carry out their original plans. They left for the Western Hemisphere and were not heard from again for years.

## MARGARET AND THE SATURDAY NIGHT BATH

During the four years which followed my promise to my grandmother, I believed I worked harder and put in longer hours than I ever did before or after. A bright goal was always before me—I must walk those gilded streets and gather in gold with which to repay in part my grandmother for her unnumbered kindnesses and the gift of her affection. The prospect ahead was intriguing but always there was apprehension. How could I rejoin my family as a real part of the household? I had heard from the neighbors and relatives how upset my father had been when my mother became pregnant with me. What sort of welcome could I expect? Even with the constant encouragement of my grandmother, and her often-repeated assurances that a wonderful welcome awaited me beyond the sea, I was unsure about going to live with my parents.

For one thing, to obtain the money to pay for the trip to America appeared an almost impossible task. The amount required was actually equal, in that isolated community, to the pay of a robust farm hand over a twelve-year period. Yet I realized that I could not wait so long. Some way, somehow, I must cut the time to at least one-third. But in an impoverished country, laid waste by roving groups of irregulars from both armies, its population reduced by fully forty percent, its farms ravaged and its livestock destroyed or stolen, it would be difficult. It required all the persistence, all the persuasive genius of my wonderful grandmother, to keep my enthusiasm alive. My uncle, sick and nearly helpless, also had his eyes on North America. Together we planned to make the trip, he to find new health, if possible; I to join my parents and to carry out the work entrusted to me by my grandmother. The enduring courage of that poor man, his stalwart belief that somewhere beyond the sea lay a golden future for each of us, and his singly focused faith and determination, all helped me mightily during those long, seemingly endless days of labor.

I had found an opening on a farm some thirteen miles south of the village where an invalid woman and her three daughters were trying to make a living. The father had been killed in the war and the eldest girl, Margaret, had become the master of the household, as was customary. She was a most ambitious person, a driver, whose only object in life was to get things done. With the willingness of the two younger sisters to "give their all," the farm began to bring forth exceptional crops. The four of them seemed to welcome my presence and while I temporarily missed the companionship of my grandmother, I soon fell into their routine.

That was the beginning. I became a sort of assistant to Margaret. She seemed to like my tagging along, as no task deterred me from giving to it whatever strength I possessed. In turn, this close friendship with the hard-working woman helped me immeasurably, financially as well as other ways. The first evidence was the gift to me of a runt steer—a little animal that Fate seemed to have destined to an existence of worthlessness. In the months which followed, through my careful nursing and attention, the small creature developed into a true prize-winner. The next gift was a crippled calf which benefited from my massage of its knotted muscles and became a splendid milker. Money from the sale of such animals began to mount.

As the months slowly worked on into the years, my funds rose steadily. But it was the introduction of the new German mark that enabled me to collect currency in bundles. Soon I possessed a bushel of these precious notes in an old sack hidden in the hay of the barn. Yes, as my grandmother had foretold, everything was possible through faith and hard work and I felt I would soon be on my way to the new world and the new opportunities.

Our Saturday night bath! As regular as the coming of that special day in the week! And all of us, the invalid mother, the three sisters, and I took the ablutions together in the square, unpainted building which roosted like a sentinel at the beginning of the rye field, some three hundred feet from the main house. Winter, summer, spring, and fall, it was a never-ending weekly ritual. In warm or chilly weather, in summer's heat or winter's blizzards, year in and year out, we made that inevitable journey after nightfall. That invigorating, blood tingling custom probably had much to do with our ability to toil continuously from sun up to sun down.

But our bath did not include the usual round wooden tub, the bar of hard, home-made yellow soap, and the warm kitchen. In fact, the Saturday night bath as I recall it was entirely without soap and was also minus any cloths to wipe away the grime of the fields, the dust of the threshing floor, and the ordinary stable dirt. These cleansing episodes only occurred in that square building by the rye field, a building used for no other purpose. The preparations were lengthy and the labor was supplied by the youngest sister, who was known as the "housekeeper," as a special Saturday chore which must be wedged in between her other labors.

In the middle of this ruggedly built bath house was a bed of yellow sand surrounded by board planking. In the center of this sand had been erected, years before, with much painstaking labor, an arch of great stones, balanced expertly without mortar, towering several feet into the air. These stones, originally carted from the bed of the nearby creek, had been so arranged that a great fire could be kindled at their base. If the fire was carefully fed all day Saturday with wood, by the time darkness fell the mass of rock was almost white with heat and the piles of ashes about the base were cherry red. There was no chimney in this box-like structure, but the smoke escaped through vents along the eaves. With the entrance door ajar there was plenty of draft, but even so the atmosphere inside was blazing hot, an eye-watering mixture of dust, smoke, and air.

After dark, the five of us—as devoid of raiment as were the early inhabitants of the Garden of Eden—would leave the house and make our way slowly down the path, the two younger girls helping the weakened mother. In fair or foul weather, the routine never varied. Arriving at the door, Margaret would take the lead and we would all dodge inside. The door closed with a bang and we would experience difficulty in breathing the hot air. The sand was too warm for our feet so we would range ourselves along the wall on the boards and feel for the tubs full of water we knew were there.

In silence, one after another, we would slip into our tub. Here again, Margaret would take command and armed with a heavy, stiff brush, she would go over the body of the one in the tub while we waited in the sultry atmosphere for this first ritual to come to an end. When the final bather had climbed out onto the boards, Margaret would take a gourd, dip it into a tub and with a showering swish she would send the contents over the torrid stones. The hissing which followed was terrific. The atmosphere instantly changed from hot aridity slightly tinged with wood smoke, into an enveloping cloud of hot steam which rolled outward from the stones and blotted everything from sight.

Time and again the swish of the water sounded. The pressure of the atmosphere around us seemed to increase as we stood mutely gasping for breath. The excessive heat opened our pores and the sweat tumbled in little rivulets down our arms and legs.

It was about this time that talk began to break out, coming from various directions, with only the peculiarities of the voices of each to designate the speaker's identity. It was wonderful to just stand there and feel vigor build up in the body.

As we all became more accustomed to the intense, moist atmosphere the older girls would clamber to the top bunks along the wall where the heat was actually less bearable than near the sand, where I would crouch low against the edge of the boards.

But merely enduring the hot, white, blinding, airy cloud was not sufficiently exhilarating, according to our Margaret. The long willow switches would be pulled down from the upper bunk and she would begin to lay about her in widening circles until the body of each of us was bright red.

"It is the only thing that will make your blood tingle," she would exclaim, permitting none of us to escape. However, she would finally turn the switch over to her sisters who would belabor her with equal vigor.

The Saturday night bath took a full hour and when we were ready to leave, it meant a long trip of more than three hundred feet to the back door of the farmhouse. To me, in the frigid winter, this seemed quite a chore. One of the girls would open the door slightly, reach her naked arm out, and bring in a bucket of icy water. She would often have to break the thin sheet of ice on the surface. With this "Greenland smile," as Margaret used to say, we would take turns sloshing the chilling liquid over our bodies to close the pores the tremendous heat had opened so widely. It was a distinct shock, but most exhilarating. Each one of us submitted docilely to the drenching as we knew it was our protection against colds, chills, and chest disturbances.

Even after this frigid bath, it took courage to open the door and step out into as much as a foot of snow that for months had made a white mantle in the yard. But we did it, one after another, and I early learned that by going first and dashing away toward the house while the two younger girls helped their mother, I could escape being rolled in a snow bank or having handfuls of the chilling powder thrown over my body by the laughing girls.

Yes, the Saturday night bath was an event in my life all during the four years I spent as a part of that wonderful family.

**THE EXECUTIONER**

It was toward the close of my third year of labor that I began to have visions of wealth. Our cattle at the market in the city were exchanged for new German marks in stacks and very soon the villagers, taking advantage of the wonderful flood of money, began picturing themselves living in luxury in the large cities, enjoying a deserved rest in the later years of their lives. My store of marks in the barn had grown steadily. Where once a steer brought to me a whole year's wages as a farm laborer, now even an inferior animal would bring four times that amount. In my mind I pictured myself arriving in America, not penniless, but with plenty of money to obtain that "book" education my ailing uncle spoke about so enthusiastically.

As might be expected, this strange prosperity was "catching" everywhere. The villagers began to see new opportunities; a rainbow seemed to have placed its proverbial pot of gold on each doorstep. Strangers began to appear with grip sacks full of the German money and even the most reluctant farmer could hardly hesitate to sell the plot of ground his family had held for generations when the offer was five to six times what it originally had been worth. The impetus to coast on this tide of sudden wealth passed all limits when one of the oldest, most venerated families severed its roots from the land its forebears had passed from father to son for almost a thousand years. The whispered price set tongues in motion as the man and six children packed and moved to a larger town, preparing to spend the rest of their days in luxurious surroundings, hardly even dreamed of before.

And then the crash came. My grandmother seemed to have sensed it for some weeks. In her accustomed way she learned of the disaster before others in the village. The German mark, which we had valued so highly, the bags full which I had concealed in the haymow, were worthless. I carried this terrifying secret for some time while my grandmother painstakingly worked out the truth. She was careful as always, because she knew fully what this staggering fact meant to our little world. And when the situation could no longer be held in check, I echoed her words, "God help everyone!"

I am not going to set forth the horror of the weeks which followed. I shall give but one incident of probably fifty into which I was drawn to play a part, all of them heart-tearing tragedies that were typical of the terrible dramas that were being enacted throughout Eastern Europe at that time.

There was a family which had been raised on the farm next to that where I worked. Only one child remained of the five that used to welcome me before the war ravaged the countryside. I was about eight when little Dora was born, but the others, now gone, were much older. This little girl, probably because of her loneliness, would ride over to see me in the evenings when work was completed. We would sit together in the darkness and I would let her plan what we would do (ages seemed to make no differ-ence to her) when we were in that new land across the ocean. Her three brothers had died in the war, the eldest shot in their back-yard as he tried to prevent a group of raiders from driving off their only cow. The sister, then about sixteen, had been carried away by a party of soldiers and her fate would probably always remain a mystery, along with the countless other unexplained dis-appearances with which we were all familiar. The mother, almost an invalid, grieved deeply the loss of her boys and eldest daughter. A few weeks before, the father had sold the farm to strangers for three times what it originally had been worth. Now they planned a trip to America. They hoped new scenes would partially free them from the dreadful memories which had so nearly destroyed them all. It had been a heartening respite, made up of dreams of the peaceful future which lay beyond the seas.

It was my grandmother's task to tell this family the sorrow-ful news. For them and many other villagers there would be no journey to the "promised land," no move which would alleviate the miseries of the past. Their home was gone, they were poor, and the father, who had a crippled hand, was in no condition to start all over again.

I stayed in the darkness outside our house, waiting for the return of my grandmother. In the semi-gloom her steps seemed less sure than usual and the light of the candle shining through the window fell upon her face, which appeared haggard and sorrow-ful. She was intensely moved, and sank beside me on the log with a sigh that went to the core of my heart.

Putting her arms around my shoulders, she told the story. The father, in some manner, had heard rumors of the disaster, and when she had appeared he motioned her to come outside so that he could learn the truth away from his wife. He was fearful of what my grandmother might say and he did not want the infor-mation to distress either his ailing wife or his little daughter. As he gazed off at the distant hills, he had listened carefully to what my grandmother had said, but during the recital had made no comment. When the story was concluded, he pressed my grandmother's hand, thanked her softly, and bade her Godspeed. He said he would break the news to his wife in his own way.

Grandmother ended her simple words. We sat silently in the gloom. I was stunned, and my heart ached. Although my labor of the past three years had come to nothing, I wanted to go at once to this distant household and comfort little Dora, her mother, and the father with the crippled hand. But my grandmother cautioned against this.

"Not tonight," she said sadly. "Later they will need all the sympathy we can give them. Paul must face this problem alone and God will ease the pain and anguish. Let us hope all call upon Him for aid. He alone can help."

But the next morning Big Joseph pounded on our door. Pushing aside the three girls he strode over to the brick oven on which my grandmother was sitting. He took her hands in his, and breathing rapidly he blurted out the horrible news. Paul had gone to the woodpile, picked up the axe, split his wife's head open, and killed little Dora as she tried to run. Then the crazed father, still clutching the bloody weapon, had plunged head foremost into the deep, narrow well.

**THE GIFT**

Tragedy, heartbreak, awful despair, and misery enveloped the entire countryside for many, many weeks. It is soul-wrenching to recall those dark days when the whole of Eastern Europe was shattered under the terrible conditions of financial bankruptcy. Some day, I believe, human beings will operate on a fair and just economic system, in which everyone will be adequately rewarded for his or her work, and the kind of manipulation, profiteering, and gambling which causes inflation will be unthinkable. I tried to keep up my courage, but with so much misery about me, so many broken spirits, I labored on like an automaton, alongside the three wonderful sisters. They did not try to offer sympathy with words, but sought in many little ways to lessen my discouragement, to make my lot a little brighter.

It was about six months after the tragic news first broke that I had an unexpected visit from my grandmother. She had been most understanding all through my ordeal and her strength, her limitless confidence in what the future would bring forth, and her heartening shoulder pats did more than anything else to make the drudgery endurable. But this momentous visit removed my misgivings, bolstered my inner stamina, and gave me a confidence that would be unshakable throughout life no matter where my path led or what my circumstances might be.

How well I recall that evening in all its golden sunshine! We had had an early supper, and then my grandmother, carrying a bundle, led me to the little knoll by the well where we seated ourselves on the grass. The rays of the setting sun illuminated her soft hair. She spoke in her low, rich voice, going over in detail the discouragements of the past months and my conclusion that all was lost as far as America was concerned. She praised the resolution I had exhibited in continuing my hard work, praise I did not at all feel I deserved, as I had labored dumbly—without thought, almost too stunned to know what I was doing.

Then finally she lifted the bundle to her lap, but did not open it, as she continued, "And now, Annetta, you shall learn that God never forgets. He sends his angels to help those who cannot help themselves. You are in His vineyard doing the best you can, giving your efforts to bring about that trip to America, which to you seems so far away now. Margaret tells me how you are striving to raise two goats who were abandoned as hopeless and that now they are developing in an amazing manner. That is good. He knows what you are doing, and this bundle came from America to help you."

Her wrinkled hands trembled as she undid the cord and brought to view a most gorgeous dress, nothing like the homespun I had made on the loom in the summer part of the old farmhouse, but a dress of bright colors, with shiny buttons. It could only have come from that wonderful land across the sea. I touched it for a while in silence. Then my grandmother suggested I try it on, which I did happily. Running to the bank of the nearby brook,

I looked in astonishment at the reflection I saw in the dark waters under the fading light. I could not believe the change. I heard the happy laugh of the three girls from the back door of the house. My grandmother shooed them quickly inside as I came back panting, and stood beside her, waiting for the explanation of this wonder.

"It happened this way," she said. "A good friend of mine, a little woman who went to America from this village before you were born, who lives near your parents in that far-away city, heard what has happened over here. She realizes that everything has been swept away and wants to help. She knows how you were abandoned and how she herself has prospered in America. So she sends you this dress that you may look like an American when you land, and may thereby obtain a good job more easily. And in addition . . . ."

She paused and held up in the dim light some pieces of green paper. "She also enclosed a nest egg on which you may build a new fortune, by which you may obtain a new ticket to America, thirty golden American dollars! Annetta!" Her voice became husky. We hugged each other and our tears of thankfulness blended. "You will go to America," she continued when she could speak, "and you will find your future in helping the less fortunate, as I have pictured you doing ever since I took you in my care."

## ENCOUNTER WITH A STRANGE FORCE

On a well-remembered day I reluctantly climbed into the wagon and set out for the city, some twenty miles distant, for the medical examination and the medication my uncle had assured me must be undergone before I could gain my passport and receive the steamship ticket for my trip to far-away America. But my heart was not rejoicing. I really had no desire to leave this community where I had spent most of my life. I dreaded to part with my beloved grandmother and the three girls and their devoted mother, the little group watching from the doorway to wave goodbye. I am sure it was only the thought that I would return immediately from the city and spend another week at the farm before I must say farewell that gave me the courage to make this trip. The driver, Marcus, did not seem to understand. He laughed as I brushed away the tears which streamed down my face.

Nothing unusual happened during the trip. Marcus sat silently and I did not try to make conversation. I had been over the first part of this road many times before. Our journey went through the medium-sized town where we had traded our produce at the end of each fortnight. I knew that our destination would have more houses than I had ever seen before, but my imagination had not prepared me for the many streets and the bright signs over the places of business. The bigness of the community awed me as we drove down the rutted dirt road to the house of friends where I was to pass the night.

In the medical office, with its white walls and strange odors, I answered the questions as best I knew how. I feared the needle my uncle warned me was coming, but I bared my right arm courageously. My grandmother had explained that the needle was a most necessary part of the procedure. While she was amused at my uncle's declaration that the medication would keep me forever free from ailments and would land me in the beautiful America in the best of health, she was resigned to the fact that I must undergo the ordeal.

The unpleasant happenings at the medical office faded from my mind when I viewed the fairyland of wonders which opened to me in the house where I was staying. I had never seen water coming from a pipe in the kitchen and the fact that you could have hot water by merely turning the odd little wheel on the spout was most amazing. Never before had I seen an electric light and I gazed at the glowing bulb rapturously as we ate our evening meal. I am afraid I answered my hosts' questions somewhat absentmindedly, as my mind was busy exploring this marvelous new world. It was all so fantastic!

My hostess, Sarah, carried no candle when she led me to my upstairs room, a place against the roof. My observation of this fact thrilled me into silence, as I anticipated what might now come. Sure enough, once there, with a mere flip of her hand, Sarah made one of those round glass bulbs glow brightly, lighting the little cubbyhole like day. When she had gone I sat upon the edge of the bed and watched this ball of fire. When I touched the glass I found it hot, but it did not burn my fingers as would a lamp or a candle flame. I examined it from all sides. There was certainly no place for oil, and no room for wax. Yet the light was stronger than a hundred candles.

Sleep was not possible. After the exciting experiences of the day I could not close my eyes. What wonders! I sat in ecstasy, going over each new thing I had seen and living again the splendor of this large urban community. When sounds of movement downstairs ceased, indicating the family was asleep, I waited until the moon peeped in the window, then following Sarah's instruction I twisted the little handle and the light disappeared. Quickly I turned the projection again and the glow returned in all its brilliance. I felt I had learned something and I wanted to know more, to know the secret of this strange device. Finally, I turned it off again and when the glass was cool, I tried to pull it from the wall. It would not move, but I soon discovered that by twisting it I could take it out of the hole, and twisting it back and turning the little handle would light it once more.

Soon I had the bulb on my bed and by moonlight I began to examine the hole from which I had taken it. I turned the little handle but the glass on the bed did not light. I felt for the place which must contain the oil, and ran my fingers over the rough inside surface. It was not even warm. And then a terrific blow from some invisible source suddenly sent me sprawling on the floor. Stunned, mystified, I was unable to figure out a logical explanation for the horrible, paralyzing pain which rushed through my hand and shoulder. I did not dare to try to move at first. I lay there until the moonlight, moving along the bed, glistened on the glass globe near the long pillow. Then I crawled to my knees, put the bulb on the washstand, and hid myself under the covers. I could not figure out how a mere hole in the wall could have resented so quickly and violently my harmless curiosity.

Then, as usual, comfort came in the prayers I fashioned, and as I talked with God about the strangeness of city life I relaxed and fell contentedly asleep under the feather comforter.

Soon the noise of movement below and the brightening light in my window indicated that I had slept soundly. At breakfast I said nothing of my embarrassing experience with the glowing bulb, and was happy indeed when Marcus arrived with the wagon and we could begin the long journey back to the home of the three girls and their mother.

## I AM IMMOBILIZED

But my trip back to the farm was not a happy one. I ascribed the internal disturbances of my body to my unfortunate encounter with the light demon which had struck me down. My face grew feverish, my tongue seemed to dry out, a heavy down-pulling weight made my feet feel like chunks of lead. Long before I reached the farm, old Marcus had to pull the horse to one side of the road while my insides turned upside down. The grizzled farmer laughed heartily and wondered aloud how I'd ever make the trip to America, where the ship turned somersaults every few miles through long days and nights. But I was far too sick to be concerned about his laughter or the taunt. When we finally reached the farm Margaret had to lift me from the wagon bed and carry me into the house. She explained to her excited and solicitous sisters that the journey to the city had apparently proven too much for me and without asking further questions they tucked me into my bunk beside the great brick oven. I must have gone to sleep immediately.

It seemed to be daylight when I recovered consciousness. But I could not be sure. Something was very wrong. I could not summon strength to even open my eyes, so I just lay on the bed without moving. Soon I caught the far-away sound of the daughter Ida's voice, talking in a gentle whisper. Evidently the mother was sitting in her high-backed chair by the window and I sensed, with some concern, that I was on the family bed in the main room. I lay there trying to figure out these improbable happenings.

"She's coming!" Margaret whispered in the most solemn tone I had ever heard her use. "I saw them crossing the creek by the big willow. Uncle was right behind, leading the horse. I think we had better leave, Ida. Mother, you are closer to Grandma's age and you've both been through troubles before. We'll wait in the cubbyhole until you call."

I heard the chairs scrape and there was a soft shuffling of feet as the girls retreated. Then came the gentle closing of the squeaky door and only the sobs of the mother could be heard. How long I lay tense I could not tell. But there was a new surge in my heart. My grandmother was coming! She would know what to do. My prayer went up fervidly and then in thanksgiving as the front door opened and I felt a fresh breeze on my forehead. In a moment a heavy weight landed on my chest and I felt the tongue of little Whitey, my grandmother's dog, licking my face. I tried to shout, I tried to scream. I heard the tallbacked chair bang over against the table. Then came the strangled cry of the girl's mother, "Grandmother, grandmother, look! Her arms have moved!"

In an instant, Grandmother was right beside me. The covers were whisked away and the next moment I felt my wrists being vigorously rubbed as both elderly women worked over them, weeping unrestrainedly. I did not hear the girls return, but as I opened my streaming eyes and saw them all standing there, it seemed the most glorious moment I had ever known.

Within a half-hour I was sitting up, propped with pillows, while the three girls knelt on the floor beside the bed. Later that evening, surrounded by pillows in the wide arm-chair with Whitey asleep in my lap, I ventured the idea that the cause of my "dying" was the deep, biting pain which had come from the little round hole which had held that glowing lamp in the city. But my grandmother disagreed.

"No, no, Annetta!" she said. "Electricity, which makes the glass glow so wonderfully can kill a person, but not the little "bite," as you call it, which came from the hole in the wall. It was the substance the doctor put into your arm—you had a bad reaction to it. I can only thank God that the news I received about you at the sawmill proved to be all wrong, and that you are alright."

**THE JOURNEY**

My trip to America might well be described as one exciting, thrilling adventure after another. Yet, almost without exception, each wondrous incident was followed by deep disappointment. My first disillusionment came when my uncle, after we had passed the necessary medical examinations, explained to me confidentially that he was dying of an unknown disease, which, for the payment of a sum of money, the local examining doctor had "overlooked." In addition, for a larger sum, this medical man had given my uncle several dozen small packages of powder which were guaranteed to conceal his ailment; by taking this medicine periodically during the trip, he would be enabled to fool the American doctors and be admitted as "sound physically." For the first time I learned that his trip to America was not primarily to escape the persecutions at home, as he had stated publicly to friends, but for the purpose of finding in the great hospitals of this fabulous land, a successful treatment for this disease which had baffled European doctors.

A second shock was discovering the falsehood of the enchanting travel myth that when one was once on the beautiful ocean, contentedly wrapped in a soft rug (I had laboriously woven one in the summer part of my grandmother's home), one could gaze serenely into the western skies and dream of the wonders to come.

There was no warm sunshine, no spacious lounging deck, and no bright attendants smiling upon you as the steamship agents had promised. Instead of a spotless liner, sleek as a greyhound, the steamer into which we were herded was a sort of snub-nosed tub, dirty, with peeling paint on its rust-streaked sides. I was pushed along with the other third-class passengers, lugging our heavy bags of clothing into a tiny, metal-lined room, far, far below the main deck, a dingy cavern lighted only by small round windows. The floors were dirty, the air was foul, and the bunks were without bedding of any kind.

When we were more or less settled, the meals were spread on the greasy-topped table by unfriendly, disdainful attendants who seemed to regard us as so many docile animals. Little family groups gathered together, bewildered and puzzled. Luckily I had my devoted uncle for sympathetic company during the days of hardship which followed.

From the start, the slow, ponderous, pitching tramp steamer nosed into bad weather. The sun had vanished and did not appear again for nearly two weeks. A thick, wet fog shrouded everything, making our metal-lined cave even chillier and more uncomfortable. The wind howled outside, the engines gasped and snorted, the bunks seemed to actually jump as the battered vessel floundered through the endless waves. As for me, the lunging and shaking was too much to bear and my first greasy evening meal was soon lost on the floor beside my bunk. It was my last meal during that voyage. I crouched helpless and wretched in the back of my cubbyhole, trying to avoid the spray of half-digested food which every now and then descended from the bunks above.

This was a terrible awakening from the golden dream of the past several years. Only my faith that everything would right itself, no matter how horrible events might seem at that time, kept me from becoming unbalanced as did two elderly women who were carried away by attendants. I learned later that this journey to the western world had taken twenty-three days, and that four of the voyagers had perished and been buried at sea.

In all that time I touched no other mouthful of food. Occasionally my uncle, sick and unsteady himself, would fill my jug with nasty-tasting and smelly water, which I drank out of necessity. I wondered how the poor souls, spread here and there over the floor where they had collapsed, ever managed to survive. Rain had fallen constantly. The doors to the small breathing space outside were barred, and no attempt was made to clean the filth from the corners of our quarters. The whole place reeked with decaying matter. It was a long, fearful, and heart-breaking experience. But like all ordeals, it finally came to an end. As the ship found an even keel, the heavens seemed to smile on our exhausted, sick, and dis-heartened group. We learned we were in the waters of lower New York Bay, and my uncle, swaying weakly across the room, said in a shaking voice, "We are here. America at last!"

## SOME STUNNING NEWS

As we all pressed against the rail, taking huge breaths of the fresh air, and gazing with longing at the green shrubbery on the nearby land, the engines suddenly quieted and the anchor chains rattled. Then came a long wait as inspectors came aboard and looked over each of us as though we were specimens from a strange world. It seemed hours before they left and the anchors came dripping up from the water.

By the time we reached the dock, far up the river, I had pulled on my knitted dress, washed away some of the spume and spots from my belongings, and lugged my bundle onto the covered pier. Here men in uniform inspected our tags preparatory to our trip to Ellis Island, where we were to be examined again and, we hoped, enabled to immediately enter this land of unlimited opportunity.

Unbelievable as it was, we were all laughing now, friendly and congenial. Such is the sturdiness of humankind. Our past troubles were forgotten. The trip across the ocean was a mere nightmare that had really never happened. Although my loose garment showed that I had indeed lost the eighteen pounds the scales on the pier indicated, I was enthusiastically ready to be welcomed into this glorious country, to don my store dress, and look for any gold which might be found along the wayside.

That night we slept in disordered bundles on the floor of the pier. At daybreak we were herded into the small boat which was to take us to the sorting center. I figured that by afternoon, all the formalities would be over, my family would appear to welcome me, and I would start to become an American as my grandmother wished. I was anxious to see my tiny sister, Helene, who was described so vividly in the letters my uncle had read aloud to me.

The morning was warm, the sun was shining, and we all stared in awe at the towering buildings on the shore to our left as the boat made its slow passage down the river. Surely this was a magic land, where opportunity was on every side and folks were generous and kind.

Those wonderful mountains of steel and glass, those splendid structures reaching upward into the blue morning sky, seemed united with the lower side of heaven as I looked with rapture at the extraordinary, continuously changing scene.

And then those voyagers at the front of the little boat, able to see far ahead, raised a shout of joy and recognition. Before them in the distance they could distinguish the Statue of Liberty with its lofty torch. It seemed to be a signal for all of us to express our thankfulness, our profound gratitude for this welcome to these foreign shores, this haven, this refuge, which meant so much to us after all we had been through. We began to sing a Lithuanian folk song that seemed to bring up from the depths of each of us our fervent belief that this was the end of our miseries, the heartbreaks and the frustrations of other years. They would be dissolved forever in the clear sunshine of this wonderful America. Many dropped to their knees, and with tears streaming down their cheeks, kissed the deck, ignoring the fact that it was far from clean.

It was at this moment my uncle moved up beside me, took me firmly by the arm, and pulled me against the cabin.

He was feeling his weakness under the excitement and he now took another of those powders which he hoped would carry him successfully through the inspection which we knew lay ahead.

"Annetta," he began in his gentle voice, "it is my duty to tell you something, something that breaks my heart. But your grandmother said not to mention it until we were in sight of that grand lady who towers so high above. You have come bravely through this journey. I, being ill, could help you but little. But I did all that my strength allowed and I thank God that we have come through safely. You are thinner and I am thinner, but we are now arriving in this new land, we are making our new start in life, and it becomes necessary for you to know the truth. We will be taken to this little island where they will treat us roughly. Government employees are no different in America than in Europe. We must expect to be insulted and browbeaten. To gain the meadows we must traverse the swamp. And a deeper swamp lies ahead for you than the one which will confront me. Your grandmother asked me to bring the truth to you, to prevent your receiving additional hurts, and I shall do it now.

"Your father, my brother-in-law, is a domineering man. He is a successful baker in a small town about a hundred miles from where we are now, just as your grandmother told you. The place is called Middleboro. He has become rich and is more haughty than ever. Neither your father nor your mother will be at this island to greet us. Your father has always despised me for my ailing body and only stood sponsor for my coming because he believed I was now well enough to work for him for little wages. When he sees my condition he will be enraged. But I can escape him, can obtain better employment elsewhere in this wonderful country. But you, little one, are in for bitter experiences. He still resents the fact that years ago you almost prevented his leaving Europe. But he knows that as you are his daughter you will have to work for him until you are eighteen. He'll make you work from morning until late at night and give you only the poorest kind of room and board. In not a single letter from him or your mother were you mentioned except in a note in one of your father's short letters where he referred to you, hoping "she's strong and able to work hard." Not a word of affection has come from your family. Your wonderful grandmother, knowing how much love means to you, asked me to make up the words of endearment your father is supposed to have written and how deeply your mother missed you. Your grandmother knew you would not come if you knew the truth, but she believed it was best for you, that there was important work for you to do over here. You must be brave, Annetta. You and I are stepping into a difficult situation when we arrive in Middleboro. It is a distressing situation which you must try to endure until you are eighteen, when you will be free. I will try to stick close to comfort you and help you in every way possible. Your grandmother asked me, with tears in her eyes, to beg your forgiveness. She felt that you should be deceived or you would refuse to make this journey, I am sorry," and his voice faltered, "but you have to know the truth."

Although I was stunned and my heart was breaking, I put my arms about this suffering, unhappy uncle of mine and tried to bring him a bit of comfort in his misery. I spoke soothing words, but I was torn apart inside. The whole picture of my future in this beautiful country had been wiped out, completely destroyed. Resented, unwanted except for the labor I could perform! The sunshine came to me through a mist, the excited talk all around me was unintelligible, and for the moment I reached the utmost depth of anguish.

Then the face of my kindly grandmother—smiling, affectionate, loving—appeared for an instant against my uncle's spotted coat, and my confidence took me on a mighty journey upward in a flash. I kissed the pale face before me, grasped his thin hand and said, "Just the same, we'll face this new world together. We'll prove faithful to those who found comfort in the thought that we would win. It does not matter what troubles come to us, what barriers we may face, we will overcome them, and in this magnificent new country the hopes which we couldn't make come true in Europe will be fulfilled a thousand times. Let's look at this welcoming woman looming in the skies above us. Let us pray that we may be worthy of what she expects us to be."

My uncle slowly pulled himself up from the deck where he had sunk in his despondency and reached for my hand. As we pressed against the crowd that lined the rail we stood together, and though there were still tears on our faces, we looked to the future with hope.

### TEMPORARY LOSS

The stay on the little island, under the shadow of the Statue of Liberty in New York harbor, was not a brief afternoon as we had anticipated. For two weeks we were held there, eating unsavory food, which was thrown on the tables as if we were undeserving of respectful treatment. We were never asked to comply with requests, the guards merely grabbed our arms and shoved us along to one or another ordeal. On our arrival at the small pier, we were pushed into disinfecting rooms, stripped, and "deloused." There was no kindness, no friendly understanding. Everything went ahead with impersonal, army-like precision. Then, waiting hopefully for release, we learned there would be a period of waiting perhaps for weeks, to see if any of the immigrants developed disease symptoms which were considered contagious.

We were permitted to walk about the tiny island and could look longingly across the bay toward the towering building that made up the skyline to the north, as we hoped for an early deliverance. But the days passed slowly and the trials continued. I could divine from my uncle's silence that he was having a most uncertain time. The long wait had diminished his strength, and he sometimes seemed too weak to stand. The change in his demeanor convinced me that he was beginning to doubt that the powders, with which the European doctor had provided him, would conceal his true health condition. However, I did not mention the matter and I tried in every way to cheer him. As I now knew, nobody would arrive to greet us. All about were immigrants being welcomed by fond relatives and friends. There were many loving reunions after years and years of separation and these animated celebrations brought our isolation to us more emphatically.

One Thursday morning, an attendant with a red face came up to me as I was sitting on the grass near the side of the building. He demanded that I come inside for a "conference." When we arrived in the small room there was another official, tall and extremely thin, sitting behind a desk. Also present was a stout nurse, who up to this time had ignored me completely. The thin attendant took a paper from his pocket and in deep, loud tones informed me that I was infected with lice and that the doctors had ordered that my long hair be cut from my head as a health precaution.

I could not believe what I heard. When he repeated the announcement I began to cry and asked that I be taken to the doctor who had issued that order. Even if I had had lice, which I did not, I knew how easily we had rid ourselves of them in Europe. The idea of cutting off the long chestnut tresses that reached far below my waist was simply unthinkable. But my protests had no effect. Although I struggled with all the strength I had, the fat nurse and the first attendant held me while the angular official went over my head with a pair of clippers. It was terrible. I was dismayed beyond description. How like a scarecrow I would look if I were admitted to this island of the free. I fell to the floor sobbing, sensing rather than seeing that the thin man in charge gathered my hair carefully in a shoebox and went out, leaving the nurse standing before the door to prevent my leaving.

It was probably an hour later that I recovered my composure sufficiently for the nurse to let me out into the sunlight. But I moved about in a nightmare. I could not force the picture from my mind of how I would look in far-away Middleboro, with my head as bald as that of a convict. I tried to pray as I lay on the soft grass, begging God for guidance in this moment of darkness. My uncle sat beside me but wisely said nothing, being assured I would understand his sympathy.

I fell asleep and the shadows of evening were all about as I opened my eyes. A strange comfort had flooded my heart. Even the striped towel, which had slipped down from my shaven head, did not seem so distasteful. And when I felt the light pat on my shoulder, I realized that my devoted uncle had stayed close to my side the entire afternoon. Now he spoke softly telling of two other girls who had suffered the same loss. I was glad to be able to press my cheek against his hand and assure him that I knew everything would come out all right.

Two days later I was angry at all of the attendants when I learned that a lock of hair such as mine would bring forty dollars or more in the New York market!

## FAMILY LIFE

Middleboro, Massachusetts! After the towns and cities I had seen in Europe this community seemed wonderful indeed. There were many motor cars and the folks I met on the street were kind and friendly. After the trying weeks on Ellis Island, with its rude and cruel guards, its rigid rules, and unappetizing food, this New England town was a paradise.

Our reception by my parents, as visualized by my uncle, was even colder than he had pictured. But because of the memory of the miseries we had endured on our long trip and at the gateway to this land of freedom, right under the shadow of the towering Statue of Liberty, we both carried our introduction into this section of rural Massachusetts with a smiling good nature which did not really reflect our feelings. I had to admit that I was the "scarecrow" at which my father laughed so long and openly.

And when he learned how my uncle had been slipped through the inspection at Ellis Island, he seemed much amused. What had occurred was that the officials, after discovering my uncle's true condition, were agreeable to overlooking that little situation when my uncle "found" in a sewed-up portion of his garments a little over one hundred American dollars.

"So they let you, a weakling, through to feed on my bounty," he chuckled. "Well, I'm hiring no skeleton here. Your little plan will not work, my cunning brother-in-law. If the health authorities of this town should discover you in my bakery, they'd shut me up immediately. No, you'll have to work elsewhere."

But my uncle was prepared for this. He simply said, "I already have a job, treating hides in your local shoe factory, just as I did in the old country. I made sure of that before I left Europe. I'll pay you well for my bed and board,"

"That you will," was the reply. Then my father turned to me with a frown. "I didn't expect a pint-sized thing with a shaven head, but I'll find a place for you. And remember, you are my daughter. I expect you to prove yourself worthy of the family. Be at the bakeroom at three tomorrow morning and I'll put you to work on the delivery wagon, just as soon as I get rid of that worthless driver. So get your dinner, and wear a wool cap over your head until you can raise some hair. Don't let the horse see that billiard ball dome of yours or he'll run away." He guffawed again and continued, "Now your mother will get you some supper. And remember three is three on the dot."

That was the beginning of the days, the weeks, and the months of drudgery. I worked from daylight to midnight, sometimes seven days a week, for my board and the bunk under the shingle roof in the attic. I longed to have the ability my uncle had, to move about freely as he pleased. But I was reminded, "You are my daughter. You must do as I say or I will send you back."

Everything about which my uncle had warned me was true. My mother was a silent ghost. I felt she resented the treatment given me and would have helped me in various ways if she had dared. But my father was easily angered and did not hesitate to beat anyone who dared to question his wishes. Every word he uttered was undisputed law in the household, though outside the story was very different. Neighbors jeered him, and the neighborhood children smeared mud on his shop windows.

My life was full of strain. My wages were nil, my father claiming that room and board was sufficient pay for my fifteen hours of labor daily. Instead of glorious opportunity, I found oppression of the most degrading type. Only the presence of my younger sister and my uncle made life endurable. My sister would come up to my cubbyhole after the family was in bed. And my uncle was always ready to do whatever he could for me.

Sometimes I would obtain money from helping the stores display our wares, and when I had enough to buy a ticket at the local movie theater just down the street, I would climb out of my second story window at the first opportunity, slide down the rainpipe, and enjoy the luxury of experiencing secondhand the exotic life in Hollywood. Occasionally, my father would catch me on these excursions, and although I was now seventeen, he would beat me. My mother never dared to interfere.

Working hard in the bakery and tending the horse with which I made delivery of bread at factories and other places, was not my most difficult task. My father raised hogs in a little building on the other side of town, just outside the limits. As regularly as the crowing of the cock, every morning in full daylight, I had to push a two-wheeled cart loaded with two large open barrels of slop through the main street of Middleboro for those mud-wallowing creatures. In these later days, that humiliating chore seems rather amusing, but I can still feel the deep hurt of that experience and the other conditions of my life in that first year in Massachusetts.

But in spite of the hardships of my life, a new independence was building up within my small body. I was gradually learning how to become an American. Fascinated, I watched the happy workers about the doorways of the factories, heard their cheerful quips, and saw their rough horse-play. I had begun to understand these new surroundings and to realize that my father's domineering ways were European, not American. I longed to dress as American girls did, have "Sunday" clothes, and perhaps find some boy who could appreciate what had caused my short hair, which I now curled tightly to my head.

I was beginning to fill out physically. My arms became rounder. But soon, strange, unhealthy conditions seemed to overtake my body. I found that my stomach was often upset. Many times I would pretend to be resting by the roadside so that nobody would notice me when I would vomit. Pimples began to break the evenness of my face and boils began to appear under my arms and along the back of my neck. Even the soft food I was eating burned my gums and brought blood to the surfaces around my teeth. In the end, disheartened and racked by toothaches, I sought a local dentist without consulting my father. The dentist removed four of my back teeth as having rotted too much to save. Yet when I had arrived in America, there was not a cavity in my mouth, and my teeth were perfectly aligned, thanks to the care of my grandmother. Perhaps that disaster of losing my four back teeth (my grandmother had a perfect set despite her age) made me realize that the wonderful-tasting food of America was not healthful. For the first time I began to understand what the old men, friends of mine along the route to the hogpens, meant when they said I would soon wish the coarse dark bread of Europe was the staple article of food in Middleboro. The freshly threshed and ground whole grain, made into sunbaked, chewy, flavorful loaves; and the freshly made butter from raw goat's milk, had contained something vital to health that was missing from the soft, sweet, white breads and pastries of America.

It was a dismal awakening, another dream shattered, but one I could comprehend. It made me more and more dissatisfied with my situation. I began to yearn for the education other girls of my age were getting and which had been denied me. My father had derided my mother's suggestion of night school for me and that had ended the matter in our household.

But I had reached a point where I rebelled more and more against my father's unreasonable demands. I did not dare oppose him openly because I was not sure of my freedom even though now I had passed my eighteenth year.

I believed he might, through his influence in the town, have means of putting me in jail if he chose to do so. But luckily, along the route to the pigpen, I made the acquaintance of a retired school teacher who seemed to be interested in my problems and had a most understanding and sympathetic attitude.

I would often stop and talk with her. She was familiar with the law, and assured me many times that my father could not beat me now that I was eighteen and encouraged me to find work elsewhere. I did not tell her that my father beat me any time he felt irritated, whether I was eighteen or not. She was very cooperative. She was pleased that I wanted to learn to read and write and we worked out a plan that enabled her to help me. I would deliver the food to the pigpens on the run and would have a half-hour each morning to spend in her house without anyone knowing about it. It was a thrilling experience for me, a real adventure, and her moral support gradually built up my determination to change matters.

## AN INDEPENDENT DECISION

Probably one of the most agonizing periods in my whole existence in America occurred while I was working as a driver for my father's bake shop in Middleboro. In those days the motive power for small businesses was the faithful Dobbin, which had been displaced in large enterprises by motor trucks. The particular animal that pulled my wagon, a horse which had been abused all its life, was most difficult to handle. I had had several narrow escapes when it had taken the bit in its teeth and started to run. The climax came one day when a roaring motor truck suddenly appeared from a side road. This time the old horse, terrified, took off so fast the guiding line broke, and the wagon weaved a precarious way down the sandy road. When the frantic animal leaped a side ditch, the rickety vehicle went over like an avalanche and I was pinned under the upset bed. I do not member much of what happened immediately after that. I recovered consciousness in the Middleboro hospital where I learned that both my legs had been broken just above the ankles.

Then followed days of pain and anguish, when I was forced to eat the food that was given me in the hospital even though it sickened me. Many times my shattered legs were inspected by groups of medical specialists. When swellings began to appear above the casts, the bandages were removed, and I learned that gangrene had set in.

There were hurried conferences with my father. He finally had my mother come to the hospital to break the news that both my legs would have to be amputated below the knees, or I would surely die. I had expected this. I had seen many gangrene sufferers among the wounded German and Russian soldiers who were billeted temporarily in my grandmother's house in Europe. I knew the consequences of this terrible condition when neglected, but I had also witnessed recoveries brought about by the care of my grandmother when she was able to provide her own methods of relief, rather than those of the medical doctors. I had also talked with many unfortunates, taken away to the great hospitals in the distant cities, who had come back minus arms and legs.

At first I was puzzled at the attitude of the doctors and my mother. They wanted me to give consent to the operation, though I knew that my father had already done so. But a little nurse, a kindly, elderly woman, whispered encouragingly that since I was eighteen my father's word was no longer supreme. I realized at last that what the teacher had said was true. My days of oppression were over. I was a free agent.

This news gave me a tremendous lift. My hopelessness disappeared and my refusal to have the operation was loud and explicit. My mother wept bitterly. She seemed more disturbed that she would have to go home to face my father with my decision, than at the thought of my inevitable death, which the doctors had foretold if I would not consent to the removal of my feet.

But my position was not an easy one. Three doctors came to my cot in the hospital and detailed all the horrors and suffering that gangrene occasioned. But I prayed silently, and although the pain in my legs was almost unbearable, my resolution was unshaken. Obviously distressed, they turned away, saying I was committing myself to a slow, agonizing death by inches, and that hell could hardly equal what I was in for. I thanked them for their interest, turned the upper part of my body to the wall, and prayed that God would not desert me in this hour of affliction.

## SUNLIGHT, GRASS, AND A WHITE PUPPY

Following my final refusal to have my feet amputated just above the ankles, I found that people at the hospital seemed less friendly. Neither doctors nor nurses came to my bedside and before breakfast the next morning I was loaded on a stretcher, taken downstairs to a waiting ambulance, and whisked away to my father's house.

My homecoming was not a happy one. Neither my father nor my mother would come near me, and only with the help of my uncle would I find something for my breakfast. I will always remember my uncle in my prayers. He now realized fully he was doomed. Yet before he left for his work in the factory each morning, he would carry me out into the yard, where he deposited me on a long bench in the sunshine. Luckily for me the summer was warm, yet the sun was not too scorchingly hot. But I could not move and the pain was terrible.

I could not stand any covering on my diseased legs, so for hours I lay there, sometimes gazing down at the ring of greenish-blue which showed in the flesh just above the ankles, indicating plainly that the gangrenous organisms were slowly but surely increasing. Perhaps this undisturbed quiet through the long days was good for me. A new faith seemed to well up from within, and while I watched the "creeping death"—as my uncle sorrowfully called it—inching up both legs, I felt I was not going to die. The spirit of my grandmother seemed ever at my side, counseling me not to despair.

I tried to eat everything green I could find. But my uncle refused to search for possible herbs. He was fearful that through his ignorance he would bring me poisoned vegetation. He did give me flowers, which I would consume ravenously after he left me in the morning. Also, by reaching down beside the bench I was able to fill my stomach with ordinary grass, which my grandmother believed held every nutrient required for human health. And so, through the long days, I was able to obtain the kind of food which my body seemed to need; that is, both fresh from the earth and untreated with heat. By having my uncle move the bench around the yard on my plea that the sun would reach me better, I was able to supply my body with fresh grass each day.

And then another thing happened which I must relate. For several months I had a devoted friend, a little white puppy which gave me the affection I had missed from my family. This little dog was a regular visitor. He would sit by the hour, close to the bench, often looking up at me. This little animal allowed me to fondle and love him, but he never attempted to jump upon the lower end of the bench or in any manner approach the injured portion of my body.

One bright Sunday morning, a strange thing occurred. As usual, I had prayed a good portion of the night for relief from the anguish I was suffering. My uncle had gone to church and the family was in the bakery. To my surprise, this white puppy climbed carefully onto the end of the bench, and reaching over my bare feet, began to lick the gangrenous, pus-laden wounds. My first thought was for the animal's safety. I impulsively raised my arm to move it away, when the injunction of my grandmother came to mind so distinctly I could almost hear her voice, "Instinct-guided creatures, left to themselves, do not make mistakes. They are closer to God than any human being." So I lay back and let the puppy have its way, and strange as it may seem I felt more comfortable. I tried, and was able to lift myself to a sitting position, something I had not been able to do up till now.

Thereafter, the puppy continued its "treatment" each morning and afternoon, as though on a fixed schedule. And as the days passed, my pain seemed to become more and more endurable. The gangrenous condition appeared less angry, and when a neighbor, a kindly surgeon, stopped by to say hello one morning, he surveyed my exposed legs carefully. Then, he lightly pushed at the flesh about the wounds with his finger tips. He cut a little portion of the greenish, pus-laden flesh away. I felt no pain of any kind as his knife bit into the wound. He looked at it carefully and then, opening the back of his pocket watch, he put it inside and left.

The next morning he was back again, puzzled and evidently pleased. He asked if I had been taking any medication and when he heard of my grass, flower, and leaf diet he looked thoughtful. This time he cut away a larger portion of the wound, wrapping it in several thicknesses of waxed paper which he had brought.

It was my little sister who was the bearer of the cheering news. She crept up to see me in my tiny room one evening after dark. "Annetta," she said, "the doctor with the gray whiskers was talking with father. He thinks you are getting well. Father won't believe him, but I do. Those sores don't smell like they did."

That was the beginning of the new era. I continued to improve, much to the surprise of the young physician who had tended me in the hospital and who now came to see me for the first time. My wounds had turned pinkish, and although I could put no weight upon my legs, the pain had almost vanished. With the young hospital surgeon was the "doctor with the gray whiskers," as my sister had called him. Together they inspected my legs. Finally, they conferred together in low tones and told me they had decided to tell my father I was recovering. They called him from the house. He listened impatiently, and the information seemed to infuriate him.

He could not understand or accept that he had been wrong in his decision to have my feet removed.

It was several months before the wounds were completely healed and I was able to get about on the crutches my uncle provided. I was induced to return to the Middleboro Hospital for the doctors to see. They made no comment, merely shaking their heads as they inspected the X-ray films which showed that the bones had knitted firmly. All signs of gangrene had vanished.

What enabled Mother Nature to bring my ordeal to such wonderful conclusion? I do not try to analyze the causes. I am only infinitely grateful for the aid of my uncle, who carried me into the sunshine each day despite the terrific pain of his cancer; infinitely grateful for the many flowers he brought me, which I ate along with the grass growing by my bench; and infinitely grateful for the assistance which the licking tongue of the little white dog may have provided. As a result of the cooperative action of all these things, I have two strong feet today.

# CHAPTER THREE

# Doors, Closed and Open

**RUNAWAY!**

As I look back upon my experience in Middleboro, I feel that my running away was the only plan that could have worked successfully. My father was relentless, and if he had known where I had gone, anything might have happened. So without taking any of my belongings, one morning at three o'clock I left my cubbyhole and turned my face toward the city of Brockton, of which I had heard. I would not see my parents again for many years. The year before I had met a woman who said she lived in Brockton. Out of kindness she had suggested she would like to have me visit her if such a thing were possible. I did not know her name, or the number of the house where she lived, but I felt that if I reached that street in Brockton, she would be at the door to greet me.

It was late that afternoon when I found the street and began going from house to house, searching for her. I did not doubt for an instant that she would eventually answer my knock on the front door, but I left at least a mile of puzzled householders before her smiling face appeared behind the screen door and she welcomed me into her dining room.

Together we found a job in a factory paying me three dollars a week, which the woman accepted for my room and board. I will not dwell upon the four years which followed. My skill as a factory worker increased and soon I was mailing substantial sums of cash to my grandmother in Europe each week. Strangely, I never received a single word in response. As I became acquainted with American ways, I was able to learn what was happening in Middleboro. When I heard that my uncle had returned to Europe to die, I sent him a note, begging him to see my grandmother and ask if she would write me at least one letter. I did not receive a direct reply to this note, but about four months later, a letter came from Europe containing an explanation from my uncle. At the time, what he wrote seemed the greatest blow I could possibly be called upon to endure. I do not have that letter now, but I recall every burning word. Only my deep faith permitted me to receive this blow and somehow survive it. My uncle wrote:

"Annetta: Dear little orphan—I am home. My strength is almost gone and this is probably the last communication I shall ever put on paper. Your grandmother passed on last week. Poor soul—she now knows the truth because she found the doors of heaven open and learned quickly of the great sacrifices made by a little girl in far-away America. Your wonderful grandmother, as you so lovingly called her, never received a penny of the vast sums you mailed to her through the years. Her daughter-in-law Ellen, with whom she lived and who is now grudgingly caring for me, took the money you sent each week and never mentioned that anything had come from America. I was in a terrible position, on the bounty of Ellen, and while I talked with your grandmother before she went to her Maker, I did not dare to tell her the truth."

"Do not worry, Annetta, your grandmother knows the truth about the money you slaved for and sent. But its failure to get into her hands made no difference. She blessed you with her last words and passed on in her sleep. Please feel that she is ever at your shoulder now, as I shall be when God ends this cruel pain in my neck and shoulders and takes me. May my own good God keep you safely until I can join Grandmother, who is already at your side.

Your loving Uncle, Frank."

**MARRIAGE**

For a while I worked in an eating establishment which was owned and operated by a very ambitious woman. She realized my extreme need for money after I had hurt my back and was forced to give up my work in the factory, and induced me to come into the business with her as her "assistant," promising that I would participate in the future profits. Due to my lack of experience I accepted, but soon discovered that this association reduced my status to virtual slavery. I worked an average of eighteen hours in each twenty-four, seven days a week.

In the end, my feet caved in and I became a cripple, so badly afflicted I could not even climb stairs. I pleaded with my employer to send me to the hospital, but she refused and offered me a stout cane to lean on. So I quit the job forthwith only to find she would not pay me a penny for my many weeks of labor or even allow her husband to drive me the long distance to a bus line where I could obtain transportation to the hospital.

It took me three hours to cover that endless expanse of road, lugging my two heavy grips. I would hobble along, dragging one suitcase a short distance. Hiding it in the bushes, I went back for the other one. But finally the task was accomplished, I stopped the bus, and arriving in the larger city I almost crawled to the hospital. Since I had no money I suggested to the doctors that if they would "fix up" my feet, I would work out the charge, whatever it might be. So in six weeks time the pains were gone, and I found I owed the hospital just short of a year of toil.

But I was happy. The surroundings were better than I had experienced any time before in this country, and the hospital authorities were most helpful. In the changed atmosphere, I began to renew my interest in helping others. I joined several little groups of dedicated persons to continue exploring the Scriptures. My future brightened materially and this new mode of life afforded the opportunity to do the things my grandmother had visualized for me.

And then I met the man who later became my husband, when he came to visit a friend who was a patient in the hospital. He was a member of an old New England family which proudly traced its roots back to an area in Great Britain that bore its name. As the only boy in a household with three doting, older sisters, his ideas of the marriage relationship were somewhat different from mine. But I was in love, and ignored the suggestions of my good friends the nurses, who, being more experienced and wiser, cautioned patience.

Our wedding was a modest one and we went to live in a small, furnished apartment near the hospital, where I continued to work. In that simple environment I was happy for a short two months when my husband's father, with whom he worked, became seriously ill. In this crisis I was prevailed upon against my better judgment to give up the apartment and go to live in the large family homestead. After a short time, I discovered that any interest I had outside the home met with the disapproval of my mother-in-law and also of her son, my husband. I was now dwelling in her house, she told me frankly, conveying also her feeling that her son's marriage had been ill-advised. In a tone which allowed no response, she gave me to understand unmistakably that I should be grateful for whatever treatment might be accorded me. She warned me to leave religion to the ministers and become a "proper housewife," as my husband was insisting.

So I became her "assistant" and under the working out of the usual New England traditions of housewifery, all my other yearnings appeared to be permanently suppressed. But this did not seem altogether strange to me. As a child in Europe I had observed that the average wife was merely an inarticulate chattel.

The situation did not change until, after eleven years of marriage, my little girl was born. As I look back, this event was the real beginning of the final breakup of my marriage. My husband resented the fact that I had not given birth to a boy, and showed his dislike for the baby in so many ways that it aroused my deepest concern. I am sure that the buffer presence of my mother-in-law prevented an open break at the time.

Yet, despite the inner turmoil, which was a part of my daily life, reason was beginning to penetrate into my confused mind. I began to realize that I, as an individual human being, had a right to my own beliefs and interests. It was during this gradual awakening that the passing of my mother-in-law occurred. In the readjustments which followed, the restraints that had bound me in bands of tradition began to loosen. My husband stopped opposing my outside activities and this permitted me to become a happy volunteer worker in one of the largest charities in New England.

This, in turn, brought the opportunity whereby my interest in religion began to find expression once again.

As my vision broadened and I began to understand the place of women in America, I discovered that my suppression was not a general characteristic of all married women's status. I worked with many women, who, while being good housewives, wholeheartedly helped those who needed it, with the full encouragement of their husbands. Instead of looking upon their wives' efforts with disdain, I learned that many husbands approved their endeavors and were glad of their accomplishments.

## BECOME A MINISTER AND BUILD MY TEMPLES

It was about this time that I became restless in my local church association, one my mother-in-law had insisted upon. I seemed to be in a straitjacket of fixed customs and beliefs, where nobody but the minister was deemed capable of interpreting the passages of the Bible, and what he propounded had to be accepted as the final word without discussion. Being a student of the Scriptures I found that sometimes the sermons were contrary to my common sense, but in the past I had been shushed into silence by my husband.

Probably another turning point came when my Sunday School class of boys was abruptly taken from me and given to an elderly spinster. Where I should merely have tested each boy on his ability to memorize the text, I had tried to show them how, in their daily lives, each could follow in the footsteps of Jesus by aiding others. I learned quickly that a Sunday School teacher must stay within the shadow cast by the local pastor, no matter how unrealistic that shadow may be.

In the talk that followed, administered in the quiet of the ministerial home by an agitated cleric, I ventured the idea that I might become a minister so that I could teach my belief of God. He laughed outright, told me that I was a married woman and advised me to "go home, be a good housewife, and let those who have been through theological schools interpret the Bible for others."

As I look back upon the situation, this incident in the home of the much-disturbed minister was probably the final activating force which drove me—contrary to the wishes of my husband—to seek broader training and laid the foundation of my later activities. No longer was I at the crossroads, wandering aimlessly; no longer was I beset with problems, seeking answers. Before me spread a grand golden boulevard to the distant horizon I longed for, a highway that was straight and direct: "Become a minister and build My temples."

I redoubled my efforts with the great New England charity, and in addition I joined a religious organization. Now that my goal was definite and plainly outlined before me, it made conditions in my home ever more hazardous. It aroused the anger of my husband to such an extent that I was forced to seek outside employment in order to purchase the textbooks which I needed, and to arrange for the taking of fall courses in the Midwest.

During this trying time my daughter was blooming into maturity, and for her sake I was determined to meet with confidence whatever crisis occurred in my home. I wanted to do whatever was necessary to keep my marital status intact until my daughter should enter college. I believed that her education was extremely important. I felt more and more the need of the school training I had missed as a growing child in Europe and which years of toil in this New World had denied me.

So I did my utmost to help my daughter. I saw to it that she had every comfort possible, and gave her the benefits derived from dancing and painting lessons. Of course, I was immensely proud when her poetry appeared in the local newspaper, a wonderful experience for us both.

**PRACTICING AND PREACHING**

During my various annual trips to the Midwest for religious study, I became involved in situations which put my faith to the test. For example, it was on my third trip to the school that I encountered the growing size of this educational-spiritual institute. Apparently, the officials of the organization lacked a feeling of personal responsibility toward their students. There was a sort of callousness, which was evidently a part of the machine-like methods which were being put into practice, a callousness which disregarded the individual in the mass effort that was being made to reach the distant goal.

The situation of which I speak involves a woman at the school. I had met her two years before, and knew a great deal of her history. She was the wife of a small farmer in Colorado and each fall, the family had been bundled into the trailer so that she might complete her studies at the school and yet carry on her household duties. For five years she had worked hard on her lessons and was eagerly looking forward to the time when she would be pronounced fully qualified to go forth as a minister and have her own church back home in Colorado. Her formal education consisted of a couple of years in a country school, but she was dedicated from head to toe with a glowing religious faith which she practiced in her daily life. Every requirement, as Jesus had enumerated them, to make her His disciple had been complied with and she but awaited the signal that would enable her officially to bring His message to all who would listen.

When this post-graduate session was about completed, she had gone confidently into the office of the school to inquire when she might expect to be given official authority to start a self-sustaining group in her community. It was during this meeting that she received a shock that almost crushed her. Later, a tearful account poured from her lips to the little knot of sympathetic friends who had gathered around her.

The official in charge had listened to her words in silence, and calling for the file covering her record at the school, thumbed hastily through the papers he found there. Then, leaning back, his hands clasped comfortably behind his head, he told her coldly and without emphasis that she might as well drop out of the school at once as her fundamental education was insufficient, in his opinion, to ever enable her to qualify as one of their approved ministers.

As I said, it was a crushing blow. She had always regarded this official as a friend. Years before, it was he who had welcomed her to the school, had listened to her hopes for the future, and had then passed over her educational background. Now, when she had been led to believe through the years that everything was progressing to a wonderful climax, this "guide" had calmly and deliberately explained to her that her painstaking efforts had been futile, since from the beginning she had been definitely and irretrievably unqualified to reach the goal.

It seems to me that it is most unfortunate that far too many theological schools are staffed by individuals, both men and women, who do not realize that the qualities needed to minister successfully, are not necessarily found in the textbooks of higher education. Many times an individual having but a rudimentary common-sense education, backed by an alert mind and a dedicated soul, may be far more capable of bringing God's message to others than some of the possessors of half a dozen college sheepskins.

That night, as a precaution, I sat in the tiny trailer, watching besides the stunned, heart-broken woman as she tossed restlessly in her sleep. I could not help but wonder through the slow-moving hours how Jesus might have felt about what had happened. I prayed that this horrible nightmare might, in some manner, end with a wonderful sunrise. But when I bade the little woman goodbye, my heart was as heavy as the one she carried in her own breast. It was only much later that I learned that this was one of the years it had been decided by the school administration to graduate only men.

## AN INTERVIEW WITH HARRY TRUMAN

It was the Honorable Harry S. Truman, the thirty-third president of the United States, who had encouraging words for me during the somewhat uncertain days of my fourth excursion to the Midwest. Our living quarters were unsatisfactory and the weather had been unseasonably bad.

What made me turn my car toward Independence, Missouri, on this exceptionally bright morning, I do not know. Perhaps it was just to get a friend away from some difficulties in which she had involved herself. Anyway, as noon was approaching, we passed the new Truman Library and I had an inspiration. I drove the car to the curb and stepped out.

"I am going to call on Mr. Truman," I announced to my companion. "Would you care to join me?"

She laughed. "No," she replied, I'll stay here and catch the pieces as they come flying through the door. I understand friend Harry is a hard person to see without an appointment. No, I'll wait for you here with salve and bandages."

The man at the reception desk was short-spoken. When he learned that I had no appointment, he told me firmly that an interview, at this time, was impossible. I likewise was firm in my request to be admitted. I told him I had come there to see Mr. Truman and I had come all the way from Boston. If he had been inclined to laugh at my insistence, that laugh never came, for Mr. Truman came into view and beckoned me into his office. I was soon seated and we spoke of many things—his good wife, his talented daughter, my work and ambitions. He was intensely interested in my childhood as a herder and my intimate knowledge of the wild things of the woods and the meadows. In closing the chat, with distinguished visitors cooling their heels in the waiting room, Mr. Truman said:

"Young lady, I like the cut of your jib. You cannot fail. Anyone who sees good in everything has a weapon that is better than all the guns ever made. You have already learned what it takes the average human being a lifetime to acquire. Your faith keeps God always on your side and with Him at your shoulder, the world must give way as you advance."

Mr. Truman's idea of the power of good coincided with my convictions. Yet not only must we see good in everything, we must feel sincerely that the good is there no matter what the circumstances may be. We must always feel inwardly that a reason exists for our puzzlement or our dilemma, and that the reason, whatever it may be, will work out for our betterment. At this moment, I cannot remember anything happening to me that did not prove helpful in the end. The ups and downs of life, if we will receive them as inevitable and strive always to better ourselves and those about us, are like a flight of stairs leading ever upward.

## SORROWFUL GOODBYE

Matters in my home had come to such a pass that the eventual break-up of my marital relationship seemed inevitable. I had tried my best to avoid an open rupture which the world was bound to misunderstand. My husband's mother had taught me one New England precept I held ever in mind: "Do not wash your dirty linen in public." For my daughter's sake I worked diligently so there would be no disruption of our home life, which seemed so serene and peaceful even to our closest neighbors. I determined to undergo any type of humiliation without protest for my daughter's sake. I wanted her to find other attachments before the real crash came. Naturally, she was familiar with the strained relations and had understood the meaning of the long periods of silence in which my husband refused to speak to either of us.

I realized fully that my husband could better provide for my daughter's future than I could, especially in these surroundings where a broken household is always blamed on the wife. Yes, I felt the break was due, but I hoped to stall it off for several years by peacefully bearing my husband's outbursts. And I prayed that my daughter could patch up the differences with her father, as he alone could meet the coming expense of a college education.

So I was unprepared for what happened. When I arrived back in Massachusetts from my fourth fall trip to the Midwest, I was confronted by a definite condition that could not be circumvented. I found the home barred to me, and my daughter had disappeared. It was several years before I saw her again.

Without a change of warm clothes except those in my suitcase and without a penny in cash, I felt as though the universe had collapsed on me. A good friend, aware of my momentary helplessness, took me temporarily into her home in Brockton. She had confidence that I would get on my feet again as soon as the blow could be counteracted by my faith in God. And she was right. My prayers were quickly answered in the form of another friend, a former neighbor in Stoughton, who requested that I go to Cape Cod to fill in for a short period as an aid to her older sister, who was slowly dying of breast cancer.

My stay lengthened into months and I found that I was a real comfort to that courageous woman whose life was slipping away. Despite excruciating pain she bore up wonderfully.

My daily trips to the post office for her mail became a fairyland routine as I played with the chipmunks along the way and enjoyed the scoldings of the birds in the nearby thickets. It brought back vividly my childhood in far-away Lithuania and the host of friends I once had among the animals of the meadows and woodlands.

The long walks along the ocean and the hours of contemplation under the trees in the yard, while the sick woman was seeking restless naps, gave me ample opportunity for self-appraisement. Each week I would drive forty miles to Boston where I taught elements of Scripture. This helped me mightily because I was able to sympathize with the troubles of others and aid them in settling problems, and in return fed the deep satisfaction of having been able to bring more happiness and contentment into the world.

Now I was no longer struggling with an intangible future, no longer in doubt as to what I would eventually do. The knot had been effectively cut by my husband, and when I had recovered my equilibrium to some degree, I started on the road my grandmother had visualized for me long ago. I would make myself worthy of the trust she had in me, unmindful of the passing of so many years during which I had been diverted from my goal.

Everyone around me was anxious to lighten my burden as they sensed the great loneliness I felt. Even after my good friend with the breast cancer had passed on, I was permitted to linger on in the white house for a full year as I prepared for the future. It was only much later that I saw my husband again. He offered to open our home to me on condition that I give up all outside activities, a condition I could not accept.

## THE "TEMPLE" IDENTIFIED

The manner of the teaching of Jesus Christ appealed to me most strongly. He built no temples, He piled no stone on stone, and His congregations were wherever He could find them, usually under the blue dome of heaven, beside the waters, in the public thoroughfares, and on the slopes of the mountains. His methods seemed to me warm, friendly, and intimate. The stately pews, and the pulpit high above the kneeling congregation, which seemed to place the devout clergyman on a plane above the dedicated believers below, were repugnant to me. I wanted always to be a part of the throng, rubbing shoulders with them, helping the suffering and offering assurances of better times to come, as one human being to another. In my appraisal of the duties of a minister, the unfortunate human being whom I could help personally, whom I could touch, whom I could comfort and encourage, was far more important than a whole church full of eager listeners who might ponder upon each word I uttered. I wanted to reach people by deeds, not words.

Elsewhere, I have gone into detail about how I received the message to "become a minister and build My temples." My present problem was how to carry out the last part of His mandate.

It was while I was living in Connecticut that a total stranger brought the key which solved the problem of just how I should carry out that part.

I had spent the winter of 1960-1961 in Connecticut with my sister where, during the day, I carried on my studies in the public libraries and in the evenings attended school in a nearby city. Once a month I would make the journey to Boston to attend a meeting of health-seekers at the home of Dr. Alonzo J. Shadman in Forest Hills, a Boston suburb. These gatherings were always inspirational. Dr. Shadman was a character, a man with a distinct personality, who was not afraid to speak what was on his mind, irrespective of who was present.

I had met this physician several years before and my admiration for his courage and ability grew as the months passed. He was a most forward-looking medical doctor, and at that time (his later years) he had abandoned surgery for what appeared to him the more favorable results of homeopathy. It is reported that during his long career he had performed over ten thousand operations on human beings, and his skill as a surgeon had brought sufferers to his hospital from all over the world. Through him I had learned much about the scientific aspect of healing and he had helped me understand more fully what had taken place in the bodies of the sufferers to whom my grandmother and I had ministered years before. So once a month I was glad to make the long journey alone over the frozen roads for those three wonderful hours in Dr. Shadman's home.

It was at one of these gatherings on a bitter cold night in February that circumstances enabled me to obtain a clear picture of what I should do to comply with the suggestion that I "build My temples." A man I had never seen before listened patiently to me as I outlined my conception of a nursing home which I had visualized was so necessary to adequately aid sufferers. I told him of my experiences during the preceding years on Cape Cod and how the whole sanitarium idea seemed to fit into the needs of afflicted humanity. This human angel heard me out and seemed impressed with my sincerity. Finally, he made comments along these lines:

"The natural health field has been my particular interest for over half a century. You seem dedicated to your religious beliefs even more strongly than to the angle of physical relief which has so vitally interested you . . . Running a nursing home, a large sanitarium, or even a health resort has so many headaches that day-to-day physical difficulties blot out other values.

"I believe you would find a more congenial atmosphere for your abundant energies in making a wider vineyard. In my opinion, churches, as we know them, fall far short of their possibilities. They seem to concentrate on the development of the soul, the "holy temple" of each individual's body. What I am trying to emphasize is that the spiritual needs, and the physical natural laws which permit the spark of God to dwell comfortably in that temple, are closely interwoven. The minister of the gospel should have a dual capacity. He should watch carefully over his congregation, both spiritually and physically, exactly as the good shepherd guides his flock each day into greener pastures, and when occasion arises helps Mother Nature deliver a new-born lamb."

He stopped speaking and looked at me intently, then continued. "I am along in years. I have watched natural healing blossom forth under the splendid leadership of dedicated pioneers. But, unfortunately, its growth resembled that of a mushroom rather than a sturdy oak. Natural healing was built on the high unselfishness of great leaders, spiritually inspired. I have hoped that those might come along who would appreciate the necessity of each human being housing his or her spark of God in a temple worthy of the preciousness of life. I have hoped for a campaign equalizing spirituality and physical betterment."

He paused and laughed. "Keep thinking about your sanitarium, live with it in your mind every day, and I'm sure you'll develop something really worthwhile. We need rest homes and sanitariums and you can leave a monument to your work as Kellogg, Post, Macfadden, and others have done. Now if you'll excuse me, I'll say goodnight and find Dr. Shadman for a little chat before I leave."

I don't remember if I thanked him. I know I sort of "found myself" standing beside the sofa looking after him as he disappeared toward the dining room where the buffet supper was being served. I was overcome. Unconsciously, this stranger—I did not even know his name—had opened for me the avenues which sent thoughts racing criss-cross in my brain. He had found the solution for the phrase that had been puzzling me for years. Now the exact meaning of that part of my revelation "and build My temples" was clear. No longer need I ponder about the mythical lofty steeples reaching to heaven, of piling stone on stone. No, I would do my utmost to rehabilitate temples of flesh and blood, human bodies, to help build and rebuild temples of the soul. Through my work I would try to enable the soul to dwell in a disease-free palace by the teaching of natural, everyday health procedures for which the individual rather than the doctor really has the final responsibility.

A dedicated soul could exist in a disintegrating temple, but how much better would that soul be, how much more could it accomplish, if that same temple were functioning properly as He had designed it to function! Yes, my mission, as I now saw it, transcended the narrow limits of a single nursing home, or even many sanatoria.

## A NEW BEGINNING

On my return from Boston, long past midnight, an almost-accident with a great truck, accompanied by the loud voice of its driver, brought me suddenly to my senses. I lifted my foot slowly from the gas pedal, nosed the car to the side of the narrow road, stopped, and turned off my lights. Wrapped in my heavy afghan, I slid into dreamland almost instantly, leaving the ice, the cold, and glowering clouds for the restful vista of a summer's afternoon back in Europe, with my dog, Star, resting his head upon my knee as I drowsily watched the sheep and goats feeding in the distance.

The first thing I saw when I woke up was the sunrise hitting the window of the car. And as though the sunrise were a catalyst for yearnings and realizations deep within my being, suddenly all of the discouragement, and all of the worry and concern disappeared. I felt great relief and peace, because all my self-concern was replaced with a vision of my mission, symbolized by the rising sun outside the car window. The voice of my God-self coming from deep within, silently spoke the words "Rising Sun Christianity." From that point on, I knew my mission, and I knew that my own personal problems would never overwhelm me again.

And, of course, I founded Rising Sun Christianity and made it a non-profit spiritual organization. It was several years, however, before I could do that, because, in many instances, Rising Sun needed to work differently from ordinary religions. Fundamental to the concept of Rising Sun Christianity, was the awareness that the physical body is the temple of God and only through healing the body was spiritual unfoldment possible. Also Rising Sun Christianity uniquely emphasized the importance of healing the whole person, physically, mentally, emotionally, and spiritually. Different from other religions, the focus was not on dogma or ritual but on releasing the power within, which allows one to handle any problem that one confronts, to learn lessons, and to never get discouraged. This was the essence of a real spirituality that avoided the dogmatic conflicts inherent in other religions. Rising Sun Christianity was not going to be a new religion but was going to be an expression of the New Age, and a source of new life for a spiritually exhausted mankind.

## DR. ALONZO J. SHADMAN

It was an early morning in February, 1961, when I once again turned my car up the steep drive to the garage of Dr. Alonzo J. Shadman. I climbed out and was welcomed at the kitchen door by his maid.

"The doctor is expecting you," she greeted me, with a smile. "He didn't approve of your driving all night, but as I couldn't get your Connecticut telephone number, he couldn't stop you. He's in the dining room waiting."

But the doctor was at the kitchen door leading into the main house. "You should be spanked," he said, as he held out both hands. "Come in and try some of this cornbread and raw wheat with which Betsy pampers me each morning. And then let me know more about what you call your great decision. Frankly, I hope it is to stop your guinea-pigging for that homeopath who has been dosing you with all manner of pills and pellets. Seriously, Ann, I haven't liked the idea of that chap using you as an experimental subject."

I laughed at his concern as he took his place at the table. "The pills haven't harmed me that I can see," I answered. "I do get dizzy at times but he instantly changes them. And I think I have been of some help in his research. And Doctor, it is that kind of help to humanity that I want to talk with you about today. This is the real purpose of my call, besides my desire to see you. So, if you will finish your breakfast I'll try this wonderful-looking cornbread Betsy is offering me. Afterwards, I'll start talking, because my ride back to Shelton early last Sunday morning seemed to have opened my eyes. I'll give you this hint—I have decided to follow your suggestion and not concentrate my efforts on a rest home."

He smiled and nodded but did not speak. And the silence remained until we were seated in his study and I told him of my new understanding of the phrase "and build My Temples,"—that instead of structures of brick and stone, it meant bodies of flesh and blood; that in place of administering to human sufferers in one or several buildings, I wished to minister on a wider scale, physical as well as spiritual.

"This is good news, Ann," he said when I paused for his reaction. "As you know, I ran a large hospital for years. No, I have put that idea the wrong way around—the hospital ran me. I was its slave. It held me in bands of iron I could not break. Always I was needed, always I must be on hand no matter how many assistants had been mustered to help. And during my entire lifetime I had the opportunity to write but one book, when I should have written twenty. In this gray head of mine is material for a hundred volumes.

"Ann, never get pushed into a straitjacket by friends who believe they are helping you. Be independent and stay that way. But do not approach the building of "My temples," with a surgeon's scalpel as circumstances forced me to do. You cannot cut parts of God's handiwork away and improve its functioning as a whole. Work only with harmless things like food and drink and forget that there are drugs and knives. I must have operated on close to ten thousand human bodies in my time. I made a reputation for myself because I had deft fingers and nerves of steel. Now I feel it would have been better had my devoted mother encouraged my interest in the pipe organ, which I love. But she wanted me to follow in the footsteps of my father, who was very well known. And as so often happens with children in many families, I found the parental influence too much to resist.

Like plenty of other young people, I capitulated and became a part of the great machine that is trying to work scientifically to better humanity. Of course, as a stripling I never tried to figure out how the human body, made perfect by the Creator, could function properly with one, two or even four organs removed. Even as a youngster I realized you couldn't do that to a watch or any type of intricate machine and have it work as smoothly."

He paused and leaned back against the cushions, half closing his eyes.

"As a surgeon I had the skill and the ability to 'take it' and I was kept busy from morning to night. I can remember one March day when I cut into the abdomens of eight different persons for eight different doctors.

"That is a rough summary of my experiences as a skilled surgeon, but since you are to approach the aid of sufferers from an utterly different direction, I can tell you now that in my opinion, many operations should never have been performed. Of course, it is true that the surgeon's skill often does save lives, especially among accident victims."

Again he stopped speaking and I did not interrupt. There was an odd catch in his voice and I did not wish to disturb his thoughts.

"It pays to think big, Ann," he said suddenly as he roused himself. "Lose your small ideas. I am glad the sanitarium and rest home plans have been given up. See the good you can accomplish, working with many, rather than devoting your time and attention to a comparative few. Had I spent my life as an author, I could have helped humanity more through creative work, instead of as a medical doctor who keeps kicking over the traces, a sort of unruly Buster Brown, as I am regarded in Massachusetts. Had I been encouraged to follow my youthful instincts I believe I would now be regarded as a real leader in health development. And that, Ann, is just what I want you to be. I expect to live many years longer and I shall sit on the sidelines contentedly feeling that the work I neglected is now being taken care of adequately by you and others of like mind."

He refused all telephone calls that morning and he had the distracted Betsy tell all visitors he was "out." As he put it, "I want to spend my whole time helping you plan the correct path to follow. You have been making trips to the Midwest each summer and I can see improvement. But Ann, do not become so indoctrinated with one set of religious beliefs that you fail to see the benefits which may be blossoming in others. All are aimed at the same goal, and the approach of each is merely by a separate path. However, jealousies exist. Each branch of this great universal march to higher things has a tendency to believe its way is the only right one. That, in my opinion, is not true. The Chinese beggar seated beside the Great Wall has much in common with the orthodox individual asking alms outside the gates to the Vatican. Make your 'vineyard,' as you call it, the four corners of this earth and no matter what you may call your organization, give your help to all.

"Soon you must figure on coming up to Boston to establish permanent headquarters. I have in mind a little project that a good friend of mine, a 'ghost editor,' is building up. For the past few years he has published a health magazine in Washington. Through him, you may be able to obtain a start in putting a foundation under your work. I am sure—"

But I broke in, "Was your Washington friend here last Saturday, the tall, gray-haired man who used to work with Bernard Macfadden, Benedict Lust, and others?"

"That's him," he replied with a laugh. "Glad you two got together. It will make the working out of my little plan much easier. This chap really has something that is most worthwhile and I mean to sell him on the idea that he needs your enthusiasm, your faith, and your determination as an essential part of making his ideas blossom like a rose. I am writing editorials for his paper now. When your wagon is hitched to this star you will find it will move progressively forward in a most satisfactory manner, of that I'm sure."

Later that same day, Dr. Shadman was successful in arranging my association as a columnist for the *Natural Health Guardian*.

A few weeks later, this good friend and advisor passed on. He over-estimated the strength in his eighty-three-year old frame and drove his car without rest from Clearwater, Florida to Forest Hills in Boston. He left the warm sunshine of the subtropics in March and suddenly found himself in an unexpected late snow of many inches, which blocked the driveway to his garage. On the following morning, still fatigued by the long trip and despite the warnings of friends, he had attempted to clear the heavy drifts from the path to his house. The exertion proved too much and he was found later, prostrate in the snow, still grasping the handle of the shovel.

He was an extraordinary man, and his wonderful influence will always remain with me, giving me inspiration to continue with my work.

## THE SEARCH

Shortly thereafter, I arrived in Boston to settle permanently. My new home was a furnished room high above the street, overlooking the broad lawn of the Christian Science cathedral. It was a lovely spot, affording me good air, and the western exposure gave me the late afternoon sun. I had looked forward to this change with eagerness. In the city I would find no mud, and no unbroken north winds, and the prospect of cheerfulness on all sides was intriguing. It was my first experience of living in a large city and unfortunately the imagined pleasures never materialized. I soon learned that a metropolis makes you feel more alone than the wide open spaces. The friendliness of a small community is missing and before you know it you become more or less sealed in your room, like a prisoner in a cage. And I found that the expenses were terrific. The amount I had mentally set aside for food scarcely made a dent in the nourishment for which my body called. Of course, I had no kitchen privileges and had to content myself with a single electric hot plate.

I forced myself to be content and set about my editorial work with all the energy I could muster. My column in the small periodical was attracting more and more attention from readers throughout the world. The plans Dr. Shadman had laid for me to eventually take over the editorial work of the publication seemed to be bearing more fruit. The publisher told me frankly that he hoped I would "work into the proposition," as he put it, but advised me to go slow and not to expect miracles. He believed it would take me a full year to "get into the harness" and while I hoped that his expectations were correct, I felt that my apprenticeship might be even longer.

But the prospective delay did not alter my objectives in the least. It was the immediate present and my unsatisfactory meals that occupied my thoughts and gave me much concern. I found that many of the city residents seemed to be ailing. Actually, almost fifty percent of the elderly women and men I would meet on the streets plodded along unsteadily on their feet or leaned on heavy canes. Everyone would have a story of personal ill health or some harrowing tale of relatives or friends battling against sickness at home or in hospitals. What was even more distressing was that nobody seemed inclined to look ahead for contentment and a serene and happy old age. Apparently, almost everyone was resigned to facing almost innumerable sieges of illness as the years progressed. Ostensibly, all were comforted by the fact that through the high-priced insurance they were buying, ample provisions would be made for their future hospitalization, doctor's fees, and nursing care. The lack of hope for the continuance of even reasonably good health in the days to come astonished me. They seemed to have no idea that the care of their body was an individual responsibility. But while I labored to gather the reins of procedure covering the publishing business into my hands, through long hours of toil each day, I could not overlook my own physical condition. My weight had fallen from 123 to 114 pounds. The simple meals I concocted on the lone electric burner in the clothes closet of my room did not contain sufficient nourishment. At the office, several people had commented about the thinness of my face. I realized that here was a situation I must remedy.

One morning, just as daybreak was beginning to show in the east and the star over the Christian Science cathedral dome was growing dim, I opened my Bible to the Book of Nehemiah in the Old Testament. There, in Chapter Nine, Verse 21, I read: "Yea, forty years didst thou sustain them in the wilderness, so that they lacked nothing; their clothes waxed not old, and their feet swelled not."

For a while I sat on my bed thinking. Never before had I given more than a cursory reading to this part of the Bible. On this morning as the first rays of the rising sun glistened on the light stonework of the cathedral dome across the street, I began to realize that there was probably an adequate answer to my malnutrition troubles. The Israelites had wandered into a section of the Arabian desert where there was no opportunity for farming, no fruit of any kind to be had—nothing apparently but brambles and barrenness, yet they had sustained themselves healthfully for forty long years. In other passages I found allusions to 'manna from heaven,' but my spiritual convictions did not permit me to believe that the Creator had sent this sustenance there after they arrived. I could not picture it coming out of the skies in showers. No, the manna which had enabled the wanderers to exist in such a wonderful fashion clearly was in that wilderness at the time of their arrival. In all probability the leaders of the Israelites had a sort of awakening, a new outlook, a comprehension that some type of vegetation, in all probability previously regarded as useless, was actually a life-sustaining form of nourishment.

A search through the libraries disclosed that there were many varieties of plants indigenous to arid countryside that brought forth, at some season of the year, a whitish flower or leaf which might easily conform with the descriptions of manna as set forth in the Old Testament. But these investigations turned my attention to weeds and the more I studied, the more I became convinced that they were the simple explanation of the Biblical manna.

Even today, weeds are separated into three groups. Down through the centuries, those which were considered to have healing properties were classified under the somewhat dignified title of "herbs." All the rest of the quick-growing, sprawling specimens of these "roadside rascals" were roughly divided into the categories "harmless" and "poisonous," and were viewed as nuisances to be destroyed. My search disclosed that weeds may be further grouped into almost countless categories, some containing tremendous quantities of various beneficial minerals; and in some mysterious manner the weeds were able to find sustenance on bleak soils that would quickly starve domesticated fruits and vegetables. The nutritional excellence of many of these hardy plants as a food for animals and human beings has been recognized for centuries. In these vagrant growths I believed I had come upon a source of nourishment that would solve my particular problem of malnutrition.

I decided to concentrate my efforts upon a few, easy-to-recognize weeds that grew in abundance everywhere. Luckily, my supply of weeds was practically unlimited. In vacant lots, close to my apartment-house home, where outcropping of rocks or piles of rubbish prevented anyone from having even a make-shift garden, I found a large variety of vegetation. These hardy growths were fighting for life against huge odds and the books told me they were loaded with nutrients.

In due time, after days of trial and error, I brought together a drink that brought vigor to my muscles, weight to my body, and alertness to my mind.

I began to realize that slavery to the kitchen stove and the sink of dirty dishes and greasy pans could be cast aside forever. The contemplation of the various possibilities my experiment had spread before me made me renew my efforts to acquire, in the shortest possible time, the ordinary business routine of the publishing office, while I continued to learn more and more about the various weeds, their nutritional possibilities, their flavors, and their many uses. Probably four-fifths of the entire land area of the earth cannot support regular crops. But much of that four-fifths is now growing grasses and weeds in abundance, weeds and grasses with vitamins, minerals, trace elements, and the other substances human beings need for health, strength, and youthfulness.

# CHAPTER FOUR

# Wheatgrass for Health

## THE BOSTON MARATHON

My first winter as a resident of Boston slowly changed to a wonderful spring. The magnolia trees on the grounds of the cathedral across the street below my window broke into early bloom and by the time the gardeners had raked the fallen petals from the lawn, April was with us bringing the famous showers and the east winds from the ocean.

It was during this month that something happened which made me aware of my own stamina in a most startling manner. It was about noon on one of those blustery, bleak days which alternate so frequently with the pleasing warmth of spring, that I stood on a corner a short distance from my room, to watch the finish of the internationally known Boston Marathon. In surprised dismay I saw those who were able to remain in the race come staggering along the pavement to the finish line, haggard, worn, and literally exhausted. Most of the contestants in the lead were thin and tall; and two, on crossing into the end zone, fell to the pavement, utterly spent.

Now I had always considered myself quite a runner. From my earliest childhood my grandmother had scolded me because I refused to quiet down to a walk. I had always driven my herd through the swamps to the far meadows at a fast trot, and as a child could outdistance any girl or boy who cared to test his running ability against mine. I simply had to keep going and that habit has never left me. When I had arrived in this country, I used to seek out the woodland near Middleboro and run for miles along the lonely roads, enjoying every moment of the exhilarating exercise.

So when I saw the worn-out condition of those athletes, who had been training for months to cover that twenty-six odd miles, and who had ended the contest in such a deplorable condition, I resolved right then that the next year would find me a contestant.

I figured that my short legs actually were an advantage instead of a detriment as so many folks seemed to think. I felt a long-legged person had actually to work harder proportionately than the shorter individual, based on what my grandmother had told me about the slowly moving pendulum in the old clock at our farmhouse home. It was her contention that gravity and other forces, perhaps partly the downward pressure of the atmosphere, made a pendulum of close to forty inches in length require a full second to cover the intervening space to regulate the working of the hands, while a short pendulum moved much faster with the same amount of pressure from the weights. Logically, it seemed to me that while long legs might reach over more ground than short legs, probably the amount of exertion required was more than that to move a shorter pair of legs for the same distance. Anyway, I wanted to test out my notion; then and there I pledged that I would use all my spare time getting my body into good condition for the call I should have to make upon it for stamina twelve months from that time.

I confess I hardly slept that night, and early the next morning I began telephoning the five great universities in and about Boston in an effort to find suitable training quarters where I would be away from curious eyes of people who probably could not understand this strange ambition which had taken possession of me. To my surprise, the idea of a woman competing in such a lengthy race seemed ridiculous to the various college athletic directors. In every instance, I found the doors closed and I quickly learned that the organization conducting the marathon would not even consider the application of a woman as a possible marathon applicant.

But despite these rebuffs, I was determined to push forward and carry out the idea. I felt that in some way I would be able to gain permission to participate in the next year's marathon. With nearly twelve months to condition my body for the event, I knew that I could prepare myself if a place were available where I could immediately start training. It was then that I recalled the sward of the long bank bordering the Boston side of the Charles River. The grassy parkway ran evenly for miles and seemed to offer an unlimited opportunity for an ever-increasing daily workout during the summer and fall. But I knew that in the daytime I would be sky-lined against the waters of the river, so I made plans to utilize the embankment before daylight each morning. The river was approximately a half-mile from my room and I figured that around two hours before daylight the intervening side streets were certain to be nearly deserted. Getting to and from this training ground almost unobserved seemed practical and simple.

Following this idea, I would leave my apartment lightly clad shortly after four o'clock each morning, and running through the almost deserted streets, I would arrive at the river bank without attracting attention. There I would conceal my coat and shoes under a convenient bush and start away on the several mile trip at a lively clip; my pocket speedometer showed me my rate was about a mile in five minutes. I realized I must better this mark. I must cut a full minute from each mile, but I was certain this could be accomplished as I hardened to the task.

The first morning I covered approximately two miles down and back. It was early May and the scent of new grass in my nostrils and the feel of the soft earth under my bare feet seemed to sprout wings on my heels. There was just the suggestion of pink in the eastern sky when I returned to my room.

Following a short nap, my rigorous day began.

That was the beginning of weeks of continuous training and, as session followed session, I extended my goals. Soon I was running a full quarter of a marathon each morning. Those sprints in the cool air were wonderful. Outward bound, the dark waters of the Charles River stretched away in mysterious blackness toward the lights of Cambridge, glistening diamonds on the mirror surface.

But I soon discovered that I was not alone. Early workers, driving their cars along the highway paralleling the river bank, made out my form in the gloom and honked their horns as they slowed their motors to keep pace with me.

One morning, however, when I went back to the bushes to pick up my shoes and coat, a police car pulled up on the grass and an officer got out. He turned his flashlight on me.

"Holy mackerel!" he called to his companion behind the wheel, "It's a girl!" In the half-light I saw him shake his head as he motioned me toward a street light. "Come over here where I can see what you look like," he chuckled. "This is rich. We have been pacing you for the past two miles, which you did in under ten minutes. What's the idea?"

I told him of my ambitions and the officer again shook his head, as his companion drove the car up closer. "This is Boston," he said. "The folks will never stand for a girl competing in the marathon. It might show that we men are weaklings. Better be sure you can get in before you waste any more time out here. And in bare feet! Lady! Lady! Are you crazy as a loon? Think of the broken bottles, and in the darkness. It makes me shiver."

I assured him I was in no danger of injury and that if I did not obtain official entrance to the marathon I would tag along just the same.

They finally drove away and I left the bank for the silent streets leading towards my room. But thereafter, in the gloom of many pre-dawn mornings, I saw familiar headlights following down the road in my wake as though to protect me. The honking of curious motorists ceased from that moment and I breathed a prayer of thanks to my new friends.

## WHEN WEEDS ARE NOT WEEDS

During that summer and early fall I covered the hills and fields surrounding Boston in my search for all types of vegetation, also working during the day at bookkeeping and letter writing, while spending most of my evenings in the studies of botany and bringing the message of better food to all who would listen. In my wanderings I had come upon an abandoned alfalfa path by the side of a railroad embankment several miles from my room. To this green mecca I would travel almost every week to gather quantities of the leaf-filled stalks, much to the surprise of several little wild rabbits, who seemed to think I was intruding on their private preserves.

For my dandelions I chose the winding paths of the Arboretum, two hundred and sixty-five acres of land (designated later as a National Historic Site), stocked with thousands of trees and shrubs from all over the world. This magnificent addition to the scientific and educational resources of Boston was made possible by such men as James Arnold, Benjamin Bussey, and the far-sighted president and fellows of Harvard College in 1872.

It was a delightful place and I felt that cleaning away the dandelions was probably a favor the management would appreciate. I must have made about fourteen separate trips to this woodland haven before I was emphatically enlightened. Returning from one of my trips I had stopped at a traffic light near the entrance to this woodland paradise and found, next to me, a prowl car of the Boston police. During the brief interval I casually inquired of the uniformed driver if gathering weeds within the confines of the Arboretum was permitted. A little while before that a kindly-looking stranger in a car, going down one of the roads beside which I was busily gathering a bag full of dandelions, had called to me a warning in a voice in which I detected suppressed horror. So I was now anxious to learn the facts. I said nothing about the two large bags of freshly-gathered dandelions which practically filled the spacious trunk of my car.

"I am not certain," the officer had replied, looking at me with a sort of quizzical expression, "but offhand I would say that had you been caught taking any sort of plant by this or another prowl car in the Arboretum, you probably would have started a chain of circumstances that would have taken you weeks to unravel in the courts. You speak of 'weeds,' but neither I nor any officer on the force would recognize the term and I doubt if the court would. Anyone disturbing anything in there is liable to fine and imprisonment and they would be sure of being caught. Only last month two boys were nabbed taking a few blossoms, not the usual kind, but from a tree that was more like a nuisance than a thing of beauty. I was in the station house when they were dragged in, both crying." He turned back to his companion and again the traffic flowed freely as I stepped on my gas pedal.

I admit I was puzzled. Dandelions were considered a nuisance on most lawns and were ruthlessly uprooted from the gardens of the folks I knew. But here was a place where man-made law converted them into something sacred. And the more I reflected on the situation the more alarmed I actually grew. For several weeks, I had made periodic trips to this cloistered Arboretum and had gathered all sorts of weeds—chicory, milkweed, shepherd's purse, and many more. And dandelions had fallen victim to my trowel from the moment they had appeared after the last snow. Other folks had watched me, and knowing the conditions, had probably wondered at my temerity, but up to this morning nobody had sought to warn me. True, I did not remember any police prowl cars during the time I was actually digging out these weeds, but I did recall meeting many of them on the winding roads of this park.

But now my source of supply was temporarily gone. The next day I started out, wondering if I could find an Elysian field where weeds were plentiful and free. I remember coming to a railroad embankment as the street turned sharply to the right and also noted the sign which read "Ann Avenue," but I was unprepared for the shortness of the lane. It suddenly ended in a thoroughfare running at right angles and diving under the embankment. But across from this main artery was an abandoned parking lot, and there spread out before my eyes, were hundreds of square feet of the most luscious weeds I had ever beheld. I had come upon a "weed paradise." Here was what I had been seeking.

## WHEATGRASS DISCOVERY

Finally, an incident arose which brought all my doubts concerning the immediate use of this almost inexhaustible weed food supply to a head. Seated in my bedroom the following evening I opened my Bible to the Book of Daniel in the Old Testament, at the Fourth Chapter, Verses 31 and 32. Here I read that the dissolute King, Nebuchadnezzar, losing his mentality and his physical well-being, was instructed by a voice from Heaven to go into the fields and "eat grass as did the oxen." The monarch followed this advice and in time regained his throne, his spirituality, and his physical health.

As I thought about this, the light for which I had been praying came to me glowing and beautiful as a wonderful birthday gift. What I had not been able to accomplish with weeds because of the long winter in the north could evidently be achieved by another type of lush vegetation. My quick reading of the Scriptural passages already had painted a golden picture and I sped along the streets toward the publishing office, elated, bright-eyed, and filled with new confidence.

## LIFE-SUSTAINING GRASSES

While I had no intention of altogether abandoning the precious weeds which had given me my real nourishment for the past twelve months and which I had brought to many people's attention, I immediately set about trying to learn more of the nutrients of grass and its other characteristics. I felt that here was something I might place beside the weeds. A telephone inquiry to the Horticultural Hall in Boston brought me the reassuring news that there were no poisonous grasses.

In many respects, this broadening of my vision was most fortunate. I knew that Dr. G.H. Earp-Thomas of High Bridge, New Jersey, was probably the leading "grass expert" of the world. He had spent a half-century in his research for the ideal grass combination for livestock. In him I had an authority whose judgment would not be questioned. So I made arrangements at once for a two-day leave from my office to visit the doctor at his laboratory. In the meantime, I suggested to our puzzled students to wait until the situation regarding the various weeds was cleared up satisfactorily and temporarily, to use harmless but nourishing grass in their drinks.

Everything considered, I welcomed the respite which a trip to High Bridge made possible. It was my first face-to-face chat with Dr. Earp-Thomas in several years. I found him hearty, enthusiastic, and eager to be of service. He expressed satisfaction that I had momentarily, at least, turned my attention away from weeds and herbs and into his "preserves" of grasses.

As I had experienced many times in this life, nothing is given on a silver platter. We have to earn each advance and overcome the difficulties. Reaching for his office encyclopedia, Dr. Earp-Thomas turned thoughtfully to the subject of grasses. Presently he showed me that there were about 4,700 known species of grasses in the world. They ranged from the 100-foot high tropical bamboo to the less than one-inch shoots found on the Arctic tundra.

"I am intrigued by your enthusiasm, Ann," he said cautiously, "but it seems to me that you have picked out for yourself a rather difficult task. Like vegetables in the gardens, some grasses must be more nutritious than others. I cannot see how the carefully culti-vated, soft lawn grass of our civilization could contain anything like the nutritional elements of the hardy grass of the Australian deserts, where it has to fight every moment of its tortured life for water. And we know the famous blue grass of Kentucky, grown on the rich, calcium-base soil, is especially effective in helping to develop the sturdiest of race horses.

"Well, Ann, during my fifty-odd years as a soil analyst in New Zealand, Canada, and the United States, my first test of a grass is to put some in my mouth and chew it to taste the flavor. Remember, grass is the only vegetation on the face of the earth that will healthfully support an animal from birth to a prime old age. I am surprised that more attention has not been given to this kind of vegetation as a food for human beings. There is an attor-ney in Kansas who, with his wife and three small children, lived for over three years exclusively on grass. I do not know what kind he used, but I will dig his name out of my files and you may write direct. Then that woman walker from England, who plans to walk from Los Angeles to New York, advertised to the world that her primary sustenance would be ordinary grass. The newspapers looked upon the story as sensational publicity-seeking and then forgot all about it.

"Please keep me informed as to every step of your progress, because I am vitally interested. You have entered my field of endeavor and I want to aid you with my half-century of experience."

To my delight, I received hundreds of varieties of seeds from every country in which *The Health Guardian* had readers. When I sorted out the piles of grass seed that had come in the mail, I found pampas seed from Argentina, buffalo grass seed from Nebraska, bamboo seed from Japan, rice from China, etc.

When the publisher visited me to view the results of the grass seed sowing experiment which I had undertaken, I had the seven most promising specimens transplanted into little flower pots on the table ready for his inspection. In many of the little squared-off sections of the seed bed, the slower-growing grasses had not even peeped above the surface of the soil. Lifting each small flower pot in turn, the publisher looked at it and remarked,

"Which one is this? It is twice as tall and thick as the others, and has unusual vitality."

"Wheat," I replied.

"Wheat!" he said. "I should have guessed it. That grain fills the store-houses of the civilized world. It is the sole agricultural product that has come down to us from the tombs of the Early Egyptians."

After finding this quick-growing, vital grass to be one of the richest in vitamins, minerals, and amino acids, I chose to work with it alone. And so wheatgrass, the green sprouts of ordinary wheat, in which Nature collects the life-giving rays of the sun, the nourishment of the air and the minerals from the water and the soil, at that time became a part of the plan. It brought into my hands a simple, home-made food beverage which subsequent events suggested was capable of helping Mother Nature to mend shattered health and to extend the span of life.

In the early summer of 1962 I took another trip to New Jersey, and I had a frank and enlightening talk with Dr. Earp-Thomas. He welcomed me enthusiastically and listened to the details of my grass seed sowing experiment. When I had concluded, he settled back in his chair with a smile.

"Your persistence brings you deserved success," he said, and with a twinkle in his eye, he added, "but I could have foretold the result of your endeavors when you were here on your previous visit. Wheat is the king of all grain foods."

He paused and a kind of regretful look came into his eyes as he gazed through the window. "It is unfortunate that the formerly good 'staff of life' has been permitted to degenerate. I shall point an accusing finger at no one, but merely state that at the present time, in the soft loaf of ordinary bread displayed enticingly in its brilliant cellophane wrapping, are foreign ingredients to cause it to stay soft longer, thus giving the illusion of freshness, substances to discourage other organisms from eating it, etc. Bread is not the only food which has lost some of its nutritive value. Much chopped meat has artificial color, flavor, decay deterrents, etc. We have no way of knowing what the long-range effect of such chemicals is on individual human beings, with their enormous range of needs and tolerances.

"No wonder this country, which supposedly raises the finest and most abundant food in the world, should be far from the most healthful. Infant mortality rates are one indicator of the health of a nation. There are a dozen or more countries with lower rates than ours." (Over twenty years have passed since my conversation with Dr. Earp-Thomas, and while these years have seen numerous improvements in maternal health care and increased awareness of the importance of healthful nutrition, as recently as 1982 there were still several countries which had a smaller number of infant deaths per thousand live births than did the United States.)

He paused and turned to me with enthusiasm. "Ann," he said, taking my hand, "in my opinion you have a great opportunity. You have been guided to the richest nutritional liquid known to man in the chlorophyll-rich juice of wheat-grass. This substance, found in the blades of newly sprouting wheat, taken freshly-gathered and fed into the human digestive system each day, will add nutritive substances vital to health that have been removed or lost from many of the foods now obtainable, foods that are often not merely days, but weeks or months old. But let me warn you of one thing—the freshly-gathered wheatgrass chlorophyll, from grass that has not lifted its first joint above the surface of the soil, is one of the most delicate liquids with which Nature has endowed us, and must be used fresh. At present the potency of bottled, capsuled, and otherwise preserved chlorophyll, available to Americans today, is considerably diminished.

"Go back to Boston, continue your experiments. Study carefully the effect of wheatgrass juice. I believe you will be astonished at the results you will see if you use only the juice from the first five to seven inches of the sprouting wheat-grass and utilize it within half an hour."

Again he paused and then rose from his desk, indicating that the interview was over.

"God bless you in your work," he said in parting. "Call upon me for whatever assistance I may be able to give. And have a safe journey home."

At the door he stopped me again. "Perhaps," he said, "and I trust it is so, bringing to the public the health-giving properties of fresh wheatgrass chlorophyll may result in partially counteracting the damage which is unquestionably being done by the chemicals which are being spread by the ton on our land. Your work is a step in the right direction for a healthier world."

## FURTHER EXPERIMENTATION

Upon my return from High Bridge, New Jersey, and my most enlightening talk with Dr. Earp-Thomas, I began to lay plans for the future testing of the wheatgrass chlorophyll drink. I was determined to work slowly, wanting to be sure of each move. It was necessary to carefully check and record each development so that the results might be published in the best, most accurate manner. My first objective was to ascertain the proper method for sprouting wheat.

I realized that my students, scattered throughout the world, would have to deal with all kinds of soil, in all stages of mineral and organic richness. I could not advocate the exclusive use of compost, leaf mold, or in fact any type of naturally rich earth. My instructions must cover the use of all grades of loam and sand and I must help my students to temporarily use these unsatisfactory mixtures as they put into practice methods whereby the earth they used could be gradually but surely enriched.

My correspondence indicated that about fifty percent of those already interested in my weed program were city dwellers who could not find space for outside gardens. Also, because this must be a year-round adventure with growing areas running from the borders of the frigid zone to the equator, indoor methods for raising the wheatgrass must be provided, to maintain health.

After several trials, I found to my surprise that the wheat grown in the shade outdoors under reflected, rather than direct, sunshine brought forth the sturdiest stalks, with better color and rootlets more matted and wide-reaching. The superiority of shade-grown wheatgrass to that where the direct sunlight beat upon it seemed evident. I also found that the juice extracted from sturdy, round-stemmed, shade-grown wheatgrass was sweeter and had a more pleasant aroma.

## THE "WHEATGRASS ROUTE"

After growing the wheatgrass indoors and preparing the juice for some three or four months, I felt sufficiently equipped with the information needed to begin thinking of testing its effectiveness. Many medical men with whom I had talked assured me of the harmlessness of wheatgrass chlorophyll, and while none of them seemed to agree that it might help restore health, all seemed certain that taking reasonable amounts of this juice, freshly made, would not complicate any ailment which might be afflicting the individual who drank it.

While my previous year was spent in experimenting with weeds and herbs, utilizing my friends and those of my acquaintances who seemed inclined to cooperate, I realized that in this era a minister of the gospel could not bring to the public at large a system for the bettering of health.

At the suggestion of a well-known New England medical doctor, who had become interested in my work, and wanted to see the effect of wheatgrass in actual operation, I confined my attention to those aging souls whose difficulties seemed beyond the aid of either drugs or surgery. By concentrating on this field we felt that I would not be infringing upon the domain of the licensed physician and if it were proven that wheatgrass could better the conditions of these unfortunates, the discovery would be an important addition to medical knowledge.

Through the assistance of a dedicated woman, Mrs. Evelyn Hoppe, I gave a little talk at a South Boston men's club where my informant assured me there were "loads of incurables just sitting around waiting to die." Much to my surprise, finding those individuals was easy. A brief announcement during my talk brought a small crowd around me a few minutes later, each one describing the reasons for his chronic ill health. Some seemed proud of their designation of being beyond help, and all were anxious to become part of the plan for their own sake and for other sufferers throughout the world. But then I described in detail the nature of the program I had worked out, using the green chlorophyll juice of the wheatgrass.

With that aim in view, I laid out what my friends later humorously called, "Ann's Wheatgrass Route." I found I could handle at least a half score of these so-called incurables each day, taking the freshly-made wheatgrass juice to their homes. Many of these unfortunate men and women were actually bedridden, weak, emaciated, and unable even to make the journey down the often rickety stairs. But I took each one in turn, talking with him, listening carefully as each recited his story, and emphasized that as long as the spark of life was still within the body, there was not only hope for improvement, but possibly permanent relief from pain.

Of course, in the beginning my words were met with skepticism, but as the weeks passed these individuals began to feel the effects of the wheatgrass. They found that their aches and discomforts were lessening, and their cynicism changed to anticipation. Instead of being something that must be endured, my daily visits became joyful occasions.

At this point, it might be well to give a bird's-eye view of my activities for the period in which I regularly visited scores of unfortunates in the city of Boston. With very few exceptions, I saw them every day, giving each one a drink of freshly-made wheat-grass juice and watching the amazing results. I use the term amazing because what was accomplished was not merely the bettering of the nourishment of these individuals—it was far more than that. There was the bringing of hope and a new interest in life to each one of these human beings, who for the most part lived on meager pensions and were putting up fights not to be thrown into some old age home to await death. My visits, showing an interest in the welfare of each, bringing a smile, a cheerful greeting, and assurance of my belief that God was also there to help, seemed to instill new courage. I was made aware of a deep awakening inside those frail bodies by the gleam which came into their eyes. It was the combination of my encouragement plus the minerals, vitamins, and trace elements in the wheatgrass juice that enabled each of them, at this late stage in their existence, to increase the strength and stamina which they had thought were gone forever.

During the year I personally ministered to dozens of these helpless, despondent human beings. As I look back upon the experience I can truthfully state that in not a single instance did this combination of physical and spiritual help fail to bring improved health.

I wish you could have been with me on one bleak October morning when I tapped on the door of a little room on the third floor of a drab brick house on Dover Street. As had been my custom for weeks, I turned the knob and prepared to slip into the dreary room to plump up the pillows of the frail patriarch on the creaking couch. A splendid surprise awaited me. The door opened as though impelled by an irresistible force, and standing in the opening, smiling proudly, was the old man who had not left his bed for a long time. It was a glorious sight! His watery eyes flashed as he held out his hand in welcome. "I dug these pants out of my suitcase," he explained, looking down at the wrinkled garment apologetically. "They ain't seen an iron in years, but I sure have got new iron or something in my blood." And he chuckled with delight.

Another example is the "Rejuvenated Musical Trio." Nearly seven years had elapsed since three highly-trained musicians, each ravaged by pain and handicapped by various diseases, dropped out of a large professional group and disappeared. Apparently their careers were over and their lifespans nearly ended. Like autumn leaves they were scattered, and all traces of each other seemed to be lost. But an amazing thing happened.

At this time the wheatgrass route included a multiple sclerosis victim. This little woman had existed miserably in bed for months. She viewed each passing day as a mere step closer to the inevitable, when I began furnishing her regularly with the wheatgrass juice. Within a month this sufferer was out of bed, taking short walks, and, for the first time in years, visited a beauty parlor. "My prayers have been answered," was her choking comment, as new hope rose within her. At the time of this wonderful improvement, there was in another part of Boston a stooped, elderly man in the throes of what is medically known as emphysema. Often gasping for breath, writhing miserably under tons of weight which seemed heaped upon his chest, he felt the dismal climax to be a mere matter of months. Here again, the wondrous combination of the nutrients of the wheatgrass juice and a new outlook seemed to work a miracle. The unfortunate man straightened his body for the first time in many years and began to walk unassisted. As he glowingly expressed it, "A new force seems to be welling up inside of me. It is wonderful." Soon, he was beginning to figure out how he could once more become productive, a condition which a few months earlier seemed to have vanished forever.

And just a few blocks away in a dismal room, the wheatgrass juice drink was being taken regularly by an arthritis sufferer, a middle-aged man with badly swollen ankles, knees, and elbows. He was unable to leave his quarters. Without friends, undernourished, his body afflicted with almost unendurable spasms of pain, the only relief seemed the inescapable doom ahead. Yet the regular drinks of wheatgrass juice, coupled with a fresh vegetable meal each evening, brought startling results in a few weeks. The man hobbled from his room, began to bask in the sunshine, and greeted his astonished acquaintances.

In his enthusiasm, he ferreted out the living quarters of the man with emphysema, whom I had mentioned. Here, to his great delight, was a friend of other days. Their reunion was a wonderful inspiration for each. In ecstasy, the arthritic pleaded with me for an opportunity to tell others of his recovery. Thus, one morning, he joined me on the daily wheatgrass route. When he met the multiple sclerosis victim he clasped her hand with a shout of delight; she was another old friend of the musical days, long gone. After seven years of individual wanderings and privations, the trio was back together again. In time, the concert pianist afflicted with emphysema, the multiple sclerotic soprano, and the arthritic basso pledged the remainder of their lives to the aid of others.

It might also be well to relate another miracle—this time, the story of a woman in her seventies, who had been a registered nurse, and who had fallen victim to ulcers that would not heal. She was a resident of a public nursing home in Boston. She had been an invalid for a long time and was so badly off her doctor and public officials were already making plans for her burial. She was suffering with ulcers in several parts of her digestive system and with running surface eruptions as follows: one an inch deep and inches across on the back of her neck and two additional oozing sores on her forehead and right arm. These had not healed in years. Convinced that what she had prayed for was near, she asked a friend to bring her a minister. In that capacity I was called. While I had been told of her serious condition, I was actually unprepared for the hopeless, helpless, disheveled sufferer I found. For weeks the poor creature had literally lived in a straitjacket, seated in a chair, her arms tied to its arms so she could not scratch her terribly itchy sores. Immovable, her life had been truly a living death.

I acted quickly. That afternoon I visited the city welfare officials and received their consent to move her to a place where I could visit her regularly and see to her comfort. An ambulance made the change the following morning. Through her adoption of the simple diet and taking the wheatgrass juice regularly, the itching was alleviated. This made possible the freeing of her arms. Her improvement, which soon became more evident, was both physical and mental. During the first week on the wheatgrass regimen she was able to sit upright and smile, the first smile in many months, according to an astonished and delighted friend. Her mental discouragement vanished. She looked ahead hopefully. Within a month the running sores on her forehead and arm healed. The angry one, an inch deep on her neck, was slowly scabbing over.

These experiences made my work that winter more than worthwhile. They enabled me to carry on this wheatgrass route in the mornings and still have the energy to work in the afternoons and evenings in the publishing office.

Of the dozens of individuals with whom I worked during those twelve busy months, most had not worked steadily for several years. Yet, as I investigated the results of these daily calls at a later date, I learned that three had found regular employment, many had part time jobs, and not a single one remained bedridden. Without exception, all were viewing the future hopefully.

So far, my mission had been successful beyond my most optimistic dreams and I looked forward to events which would help me to move forward along a much broader roadway than the limited path of the wheatgrass route.

## "THE HOMESTEAD" IS FOUNDED

For a year I had daily traveled my "wheatgrass route," taking the fresh wheatgrass juice to sufferers in sections of Boston. I now began to wonder just how I might broaden my endeavors, as I was encouraged by the results of testing this food/beverage on the elderly "incurables."

At this particular time, a good friend, a wonderful little woman living in Stoughton, Massachusetts, passed from this life. As I have recorded before, she was a dedicated soul who had given her long life to the service of others. Selflessly, she had deprived her own frail body of proper care so that she might use her scant funds for the many individuals who looked to her for help. She had been a student of nutrition, and had visualized her property as being the center of an organic gardening community where fruits and vegetables of a worthy nature might be produced for the benefit of others. She had no close heirs and several years before her passing, she had arranged to leave the ground to two friends who had assured her they would come out to her home and start an organic garden "soon." But time had gone on and no effort had been made by these men to carry out their bargain.

In the meantime, she had counseled me on my various projects and had helped me tremendously, as she had been interested in, and done research on, nutrition for close to half a century. But unfortunately she lived solely to help others, and her own body had been neglected. Although her closest friends never suspected the truth (when increasing weakness kept her in bed for five days), she had to admit the presence of a deep-seated cancer which had buried itself in her lungs.

It was only then that I understood what had happened to the great boxes of wheatgrass she had been growing through the months. The juice had been given by her to ailing neighbors, while none had entered her own disintegrating body. Yes, even to the last, she had thought of others and had ignored the "fox under her own tunic" that was eating her life away. She realized what we did not, that her sands of life were nearly spent. During the time friends were carrying on the discussion of practical help for her in some nursing home, where she would have the care she needed, she made out a will, leaving the property to the work I was doing, knowing I would gladly continue what she so proudly looked back upon.

That same afternoon she was taken to a neighboring city where a well-staffed nursing home awaited her. She smiled hopefully at parting, but three nights later, in the little room where every aid was at her disposal, she held some fresh-cut flowers to her heart and closed her eyes in sleep, never again to awaken to this life.

Her warm presence and good suggestions were sadly missed. I knew how hard it was to find an understanding soul such as she had proved to be.

Because of her wonderful understanding, this century-old farmhouse with a barn and nearly two acres of arable land was to supply the need which had been upwards in my mind for many months. Climbing countless flights of stairs to freshen up the dingy rooms of my flock, I realized keenly that their broken bodies needed sunlight and unpolluted air as well as pure, simple, fresh food (instead of the stale, processed mixtures they obtained at so many drugstore lunch counters and restaurants). In some instances, I had for weeks at a time supplied a good evening meal in addition to a daily drink of wheatgrass juice to a sufferer who was incapable of getting enough nourishment, thus giving his or her ailing body sufficient strength to pull itself into the sunshine occasionally. Later, I found that a raw vegetable salad, including buckwheat lettuce, sunflower greens, carrots, and sprouts, with a dressing made of seeds or nuts, was particularly effective.

Now that I possessed a habitation close to Boston, where I could take the worst of these chronically ill people and supervise their diet and surroundings personally, I felt that a wonderful opportunity for good had been made possible by the thoughtfulness of the dedicated woman who had passed on so suddenly. But an inspection of the house itself proved disheartening. The last tenant had surreptitiously disappeared in the night, after stripping the place of all good furniture, taking all the linens, and emptying the cabinets of table and kitchenware. The value of these articles may have seemed inconsequential to some, but the problem of replacing them to make the house habitable for several people was a huge problem for me.

As I prayed over the situation for guidance, my needs were met in abundance. Good friends and acquaintances flocked to "The Homestead," as the house came to be known, working miracles and often spending more than their resources could spare. Soon the building was re-fitted from cellar to roof. Florence, from Cambridge, painted the kitchen and helped dispose of the piles of rubbish which impeded the refurnishing work; Paul, the police lieutenant of South Boston, made a truck available for bringing to Stoughton the second-hand usable furniture which seemed to appear from all over the surrounding countryside; Evelyn, of Brookline, repapered the dingy walls, brought the soft carpeting and spent lavishly of her meager funds to supply the much-needed linen; Andrew, of Vermont, rebuilt the grape arbor and helped landscape the neglected grounds; Tony and his wife Caroline brought over house plants, and berry bushes for the garden; Samuel, of Pennsylvania, sent his mother's cherished sewing machine to aid in the rehabilitation of some of the furnishings; the Hoppes replaced the worn window cords and reset sagging doors; Walter and his good wife, from Washington, erected benches and built wheat-growing boxes. And there were many, many more who also were of great help.

It was indeed a busy six weeks of toil, with new things to be done and old things to mend. Through co-operation of the most heartwarming character, each blessed soul gave a little brightness. Through combined efforts, The Homestead became a living symbol of religious principles in action. And so on August first, this haven was ready to receive the first guests from Boston.

It was a gala opening, with the devoted helpers clustered around as Henry, Gilbert, and Clarence (they referred to themselves as the "Three Musketeers") unpacked their bundles and selected the beds on which they would sleep comfortably during their indefinite stays. We all hoped for their successful rehabilitation with care, the wheatgrass juice, and other good nourishment. Late that night I departed for my room in Boston, my heart filled with thanksgiving. At long last, I might be able to prove with these unfortunates what I had already demonstrated so well in my own body—that the regular taking of the wheatgrass juice each day, coupled with a simple, fresh food diet, would enable these elderly men to once more enjoy a measure of their one-time strength, which they had believed was gone forever.

Through the weeks which followed, it became evident that my expectation of the ambitions of elderly men springing once more into life needed revision. I had thought of The Homestead as a temporary habitation for men and women well along in years, where, through the simple menu and the regular taking of the wheatgrass juice, old bodies might receive renewed strength, and old ambitions halted momentarily by ill health might be once more alerted. I had pictured each of these guests feeling the new strength in his or her muscles and seeing the world again as an exciting challenge. I had hoped that each might swing back into a productive life, regarding the interlude as a respite in which they had become rested so that they could now re-enter the lists and win. It was a beautiful picture, the result of wishful thinking.

And so, at The Homestead, as the weeks ran into months and the Three Musketeers again found vitality and stamina, there slowly developed a situation about which even my rose-colored glasses could not deceive me. There were now six elderly men who appeared capable of being out in the world once more, but were not as anxious to do battle as they had vowed when their bodies were racked with pain and their muscles debilitated. They seemed to prefer snuggling down in the easy chairs before the TV set or reading from the many books which were piled around at convenient intervals. Their bodies had been strengthened, their minds stimulated, but the comfort of the warm house appeared to them far more inviting than facing the spring blasts outdoors and pushing into crowded buses for trips to the city.

The first few months of operation of The Homestead were not only enlightening but in some respects alarming. Folks from many sections of the country were clamoring for accommodations while the oldsters in residence, the selected six, seemed disinclined to leave the comfort of this abode which they regarded as a sort of permanent haven.

Such use of The Homestead was not my plan. It was against all that I was seeking to demonstrate with my wheat-grass regimen. I had visualized this place as a temporary human rehabilitation station which could help so-called incurables to again face the world, strengthened in both body and spirit. But the facts spread before me were plain and could not be ignored, and so, without hesitation, I altered the pattern. The Homestead became an institute, a school, a temporary home for ailing folks where they could learn by doing. I felt that even a visit for a few days, during which they became a part of the routine, might help equip them to return home more qualified to help Nature battle whatever health impairment might be afflicting them. Just a short stay could enable them to see the health potential of the wheatgrass juice and appreciate the ways and wherefores of the simple diet.

My experience up to that time had convinced me of the truth of certain fundamentals concerning ill health in both human beings and animals:

- There is an outstanding cause of many sicknesses—the lack of certain necessary nourishment. This absence results in such signals as pain, shortness of breath, chills, weakness, etc.
- While the absence of some of the essential nutrients of the body may be discerned through diagnosis, and efforts may be made to supply this lack through diet, special-purpose foods, pills, etc., the fact remains that these efforts often fail. It is essential that the causes of ill health be discovered and removed.
- The improvement in health evident in those to whom I had regularly furnished the drink made from freshly gathered, freshly juiced wheatgrass, seemed to indicate that this simple liquid food may indeed be helpful. These persons were struggling with a variety of ailments, from cancer to rheumatism. Yet in not a single instance, where the regimen was followed, was there a failure to improve.
- The foregoing conditions, which I had observed and evaluated tentatively in the beginning, convinced me that there is truth in Dr. Earp-Thomas' characterization of freshly squeezed wheatgrass juice as "the richest nutritional liquid known to man," containing a little of every nutrient needed by the body. These fundamentals explained to me why so many instances of better health resulted from the wheatgrass regimen.

## TWO HENRYS

After Henry regained his touch on the piano keys and found he no longer needed to wear glasses, one might have thought that he would give all his attention to practicing on the grand piano with a view, perhaps, of becoming a teacher. But ambition did not return with his recovered health. Henry was constantly wishing for a golden future, but was unwilling to work for it.

And then another Henry, a banker from Chicago, arrived for a stay at the almost empty Homestead when the cold weather repairing was in progress. Only the Musketeer Henry was there to welcome him. During the month that the financier from the Windy City worked to strengthen his run-down body after forty-five years of toil without a vacation, the two Henrys became well acquainted, spending their evenings together.

Henry the Musketeer had been born in Brooklyn, the son of a lawyer and a most ambitious woman. Through her influence the father's hope that the boy become a lawyer was lost as the lad was trained as a pianist. The instruction had borne good fruit. The boy had been a success on the concert stage, and money had come to him in large amounts. But some twelve years before I had met him, arthritis had shortened his career, and for six years he had been living on a stipend furnished by the Commonwealth of Massachusetts.

Through a comparison of notes, the two Henrys found that they had been born in the same month, in the same year, but approximately nine hundred miles apart. They also discovered that each was the only child in a family of German extraction and both had been influenced to a marked degree by ambitious mothers. But while Henry the Musketeer had led a pampered life and been given a costly education, Henry the banker had been pushed at an early age into a railroad job, where he had worked his way up by working long hours for a small salary. When the two Henrys met at The Homestead, Henry the Musketeer was poverty stricken, while Henry the banker was worth millions.

This meeting proved the ruination of Henry the Musketeer. He realized he was actually a has-been, a penniless ward of the state, while his "twin" was everything he was not. In that brief space of time all the remnants of his courage, determination, and ambition faded into nothingness. He tossed his wheatgrass juice into the sink and went on a long water fast, also taking copious doses of milk of magnesia each day. The result was inevitable. He was taken to the hospital by a local physician, and later transferred to a neighboring rest home. I visited him later and found a hopeless wreck, bed-ridden and extremely weak—in contrast to the other Henry, who went back to work with renewed strength.

You cannot cheat Mother Nature. There are no short cuts to health. Each of us must do those things which must be done.

## ONE BILLION BUSHELS

When I read the letter from Sister Gabriella I was jubilant. It appeared to be the opportunity for which I had been praying. Sister Gabriella lived in the jungles of East Africa. One of the sheets telling of my work with the elderly and ill in and around Boston had traveled miles from the railroad and found its way into the thickets and brambles of Uganda, and into the hands of this saintly woman. She had voluntarily cut herself off from civilization to head a camp for one hundred and fifty blighted children, ranging from sixteen-year-olds to babies hardly able to crawl. They were all victims of leprosy.

The good Sister had written immediately, asking for samples of the wheatgrass seed so that she might try it on her youngsters. They received monthly injections of drugs from the traveling doctors which seemed to arrest, but not cure, the scourge. Sister Gabriella had watched the treatment of her little charges, had noted the leprosy eating away their feet and hands, and had wondered if the disease might be a blood ailment, somewhat like cancer, and might be treated by means of diet rather than drugs. Her thought paralleled mine and I saw in helping her the possibility of aiding tens of thousands of lepers. From what wheatgrass had accomplished with all types of diseases, I was hopeful that leprosy might also respond.

I figured about forty tons of wheat would be required to give one hundred fifty children, plus the adult lepers who requested it, three drinks of fresh wheatgrass each day for a year. I did not believe a full year would be required to show what this juice and diet could accomplish in their diseased bodies, but I wanted to make a thorough test which would leave no room for doubt.

Admittedly, I was elected because I knew that the United States government, in order to keep the price of wheat from falling, had been buying surplus grain. At the time this letter from Sister Gabriella arrived, there were close to one billion bushels of this precious grain in storage in warehouses from the Atlantic to the Pacific. The Commodity Credit Corporation, the government agency which controlled this stored wheat, willingly sent shiploads of it free to countries where starvation threatened.

Since all of this was public knowledge I felt that obtaining forty tons to be sent directly to Sister Gabriella in East Africa was a good possibility. I wrote a half-dozen letters to appropriate sources in Washington, inquiring how best to approach the official of the Commodity Credit Corporation with my request for forty tons of this wheat.

To my dismay, most of these persons to whom I had written replied that obtaining seed wheat from the government store was practically impossible for an American. Several suggested that I begin by writing to my senators and representatives in Congress.

To insure a positive response I wrote to each one of the 535 members of Congress, explaining why Sister Gabriella wanted this wheat and how I would be willing to go to East Africa, supervise the growing of the wheatgrass, oversee the preparing of the wheatgrass juice, and distribute the drinks to the stricken children each day.

I received many replies, most of them saying that the writer had transferred my request to the Commodity Credit Corporation and adding that each had attached a personal endorsement of the plan. Shortly thereafter, copies of the stenotyped letter each had received from the Commodity Credit Corporation came into my hands. This communication was lengthy, carefully worded, and embodied the following thoughts:

> It was regrettable, but owing to the rules under which the wheat was purchased, none would be available for Sister Gabriella as the seed wheat and the wheat not suitable for planting had all been put into common bins.

But I did not sit around and wait for the impossible to happen. I purchased and sent two tons of wheat myself to Sister Gabriela, which she used to grow wheatgrass to feed her children, with often remarkable results. According to her letters, shortly after using the wheatgrass juice, in many cases the pain was alleviated, and the condition of their hands, feet, and skin improved steadily. Unfortunately, I could not find the funds to continue sending the wheat to Sister Gabriela. Being the loving person she was, she blessed me for having helped her to the best of my ability, and assured me she would seek out other channels for new supplies of wheat.

## THE BISHOP OF SYRIA

The Catholic Bishop of Syria, Michael Knallouf, heard in faraway Asia of the improvements in health resulting from living by the simple menu and taking wheatgrass juice. He made a trip to The Homestead to participate in our routine of learning by doing.

The Bishop had cabled us of his coming, expressing hope that a stay of at least two months at The Homestead would rejuvenate his failing body. When I met him, he appeared very weak. He was helped into my car with the aid of two other passengers, and his greeting was so low I could hardly distinguish his words. I was thankful that I had made arrangements for each of our new visitors to undergo a checkup at a cooperating medical clinic, toward which I now headed.

Within a little over an hour we were again on our way to The Homestead. Having learned that the man beside me suffered from chronic constipation, poor circulation, a painful throat condition, and weakened lungs, I was eager to see what our simple menu and the regular taking of the wheatgrass juice could do.

About ten days later I told the Bishop, who had already experienced an encouraging change in his body and was finding once again his powerful voice, about what I was trying to do. The good Bishop listened carefully and when I paused he made this comment: "We will speak of this again. But now let us consider what the simple diet and the wheatgrass has accomplished for me in less than two weeks. I arrived here much discouraged. I had consulted physicians in Europe and Asia and although several of them prescribed various types of medication, my voice continued to get weaker and the pains in my throat increased. Here my throat has eased and my voice is much improved. My constipation has almost been eliminated and new life, new ambition, new hope is rising in me. It is almost like being born again."

"But let us pass over these troubles of mine which are daily growing less and turn our attention to the woman who has made this possible. Frankly, Ann, I have learned more about health in the short time I have been at The Homestead than I learned in the long and exciting life I have led."

Two days later, around daybreak, the Bishop was asked to take a long distance telephone call from the Middle East. He was requested to return at once as he was needed at an important meeting in Damascus at 10:00 a.m. two mornings hence. There was no thought on his part other than to comply and arrangements were quickly made for a private plane in New York City to rush him to Italy, where connections for Syria would be waiting.

It was a tearful farewell. I was sorry to see him go when he was just showing the results that I was sure would blossom wonderfully into renewed health and strength. He, too, was reluctant to leave, and as we sat in the living room, just before his departure, he took my hand and spoke:

"We shall meet again. And I shall never forget what I have learned here. I shall take home to my people ideas that will seem strange to them but which will mean so much to livelihood and happiness. I am sure, after all your struggles, a new and even more rewarding existence awaits you. Know that my blessings will always surround your efforts."

### A VISITOR FROM THE SOUTH

The evening of September 26, 1961, after I had left my office, a telephone call came for me from a nurse in the New England Deaconess Hospital in Boston saying a cancer patient there had been trying to find me for a week. He had only my post office box number, could not find my name in the telephone directory, and the post office substation would not divulge the street numbers of its box holders. He feared to write me a letter, thinking I might refuse to see him. This patient was bedridden, with a paralyzed tongue, and could not speak. I assured the nurse that I would call upon him on the following morning without fail.

I visited the hospital the next day, met the patient, and learned the full story. He informed me by means of a typewriter that he had been a sufferer from neck and face cancer for about fourteen years, being now sixty-five years old. He had sought help from many sources, and finally, X-ray, radium and surgery had caused most of his jaw to disappear. He fed himself by slipping a rubber tube down his throat and pouring liquid food into a funnel at the top. In the deep South, he had found one of the sheets telling of the wheatgrass juice and was determined to try this homemade beverage. He had entered his car in Columbia, South Carolina, and though he could not drive more than a hundred miles a day, had somehow managed to make the nine hundred miles to Boston. He was then confronted by his inability to obtain my street address.

While waiting, he had consulted a prominent plastic surgeon in the hope that his jaw could be restored. The doctor informed him that no lasting surgery was possible because of his condition.

Then, through a chance telephone call the nurse had made to a friend of his some fifty miles distant, my telephone number was obtained.

On Saturday, September 29th, the man was released from the hospital. Our trip to The Homestead, seventeen miles away, was enlightening to me. I knew the surface cancer odor and during this short journey my car was filled with it. (I had nursed the sister of the remarkable woman who had bequeathed to our work the Stoughton property. This was before we knew of wheatgrass juice, and the sister had died of breast cancer.)

That evening the new visitor received four large glasses of wheatgrass juice and other juices, spaced about two hours apart. The next day, Sunday, September 30th, four more were poured into the funnel at the top of the rubber tube, and on Monday another four. Tuesday, October 2nd was a memorable day. The cancer odor had vanished from the room. Astonished, I hastily telephoned one of the leading cancer specialists in the area, told him what had occurred, and received his incredulous reaction. "It is unlikely that this could take place in so short a time. But the disappearance of the cancer odor indicates—I say indicates—the malignancy may have been halted. Please keep me informed."

The record is plain. The wheatgrass juice drinks were continued, along with the frequent application of wheat-grass poultices to the neck and face. During the second week the two deep holes in his neck, which had been exuding pus for a long time, suddenly ceased flowing.

The third week, the apparently paralyzed tongue, which had permitted only a few unintelligible words, loosened. We were able to converse.

The fourth week brought a condition I had been watching for carefully, something my friend the cancer specialist could not believe. The two neck holes of several years' standing were gradually growing smaller and now were completely scabbed over. The chalk-like flesh about them had turned pinkish and good red blood showed at the edges of the sores.

Friday morning, November 23rd, less than two months after he became a visitor at The Homestead, our guest insisted on leaving for Florida, saying he would be back in a few months. He hoped plastic surgery would be feasible, now that his condition had so improved.

Of course, we would have preferred that this man remain with us for several months longer as his stay seemed to be benefiting him so. But that decision, obviously, was for him to make.

Many months thereafter, I learned that the seemingly rejuvenated individual had returned from the South and was busily engaged in remodeling his old home in Pennsylvania. It was evident he expected to be around for quite a number of years.

### NEW BEGINNING

It was in August, 1961, shortly after I had taken possession of The Homestead, that a dispirited looking man, with drawn features and the typical chalk-like cancer skin, was brought to me by his wife. Head drooping, he sat in an easy chair, while she explained the situation.

She said that back in 1957 doctors in the Beth Israel Hospital in Boston had told them that he had leukemia. They explained he might live for a year or so through rest and very careful medical treatment. He quit work as advised, but despite that and the use of medication he had gradually failed.

She went on to say that while her husband received medication during the past few years she took him to the hospital periodically for check-ups. Yesterday she had had a terrible shock. Observing her husband's weakness, the doctors had told her privately that she must prepare for the inevitable. And in some manner, her husband had caught the import and collapsed in the car on the way home.

That night, a neighbor had given her a leaflet describing the successful use of wheatgrass and they had come to try this method. I explained that wheatgrass juice was mere nourishment, not a medicine, and could cure nothing. But it apparently helped Nature rebuild the body. I showed the woman how to grow wheatgrass, and thanking me for my gift of seed, the couple left.

About six months later, on Tuesday, February 19th, the same car stopped in my driveway and an elderly man sprang out, ran up our front steps, and burst into the house. "You don't know me," he exclaimed with a laugh, holding out his hand. "I'm the human wreck who slumped into that chair there when my wife brought me here last fall."

I could hardly believe it. The chalk-like skin was gone, he was pink-cheeked, spoke with vigor, and his eyes were shining. His wife had suggested he come to tell us that he had gone back to work the previous day, the first time in seven years. He told how his wife had planted the wheat seed the very afternoon they arrived home, and within a week was giving him four drinks of wheatgrass juice a day in addition to the other necessary dietary changes. On January 20th he had felt so good that they had gone down to the Beth Israel Hospital for a re-check. The doctors appeared puzzled by their findings.

They conceded he looked healthy, carefully studied his old charts, and examined him with interest, but made no comment.

He thanked me again and left, and on his next visit, four months later, showed continued improvement. There seemed to be no sign of leukemia.

Was that the end? Well, those same doctors at the hospital have examined him periodically since that January 20th and they admit they are still puzzled.

## OUR MARY

A number of years ago, the well-known author Jack London wrote a tragic story about a sled dog in the Far North, who, feeling the "call of the wild" deserted civilization for the hazardous existence with a roving wolf pack. This saga has much in common with the true story of "Our Mary," the white mother cat of The Homestead. Some circumstance, perhaps ill-treatment in this civilized New England community, forced her as a kitten into the safety of the brambles. Here she managed to survive by catching fish in the nearby ponds and trapping birds, rabbits, moles, and wild mice.

For more than seven years she was just a fleeting bunch of white in the distant shrubbery, allowing no one to approach within a hundred yards, and vanishing like a ghost when anyone happened upon her in the tangled patches of thorny vegetation. My acquaintance with this remarkable cat began some years ago when I visited the friend who then possessed The Homestead. I would catch a momentary glimpse of the thin white body and then it would be gone like a shadow. Food left out for her in the paths near the pond was never touched; she had apparently severed all connection with civilization. Dogs, irrespective of size or savagery, made no attempt to intrude upon her privacy.

Then, in the early Spring of 1963, she deposited three tiny kittens in a half-rotting stump in the brambles near the edge of the pond at The Homestead. It was a bleak spot, unsheltered from the rain, sleet, and snow. How this wild creature kept her tiny brood warm while she ranged the frozen countryside for food is a mystery. I discovered them one chilly, blustery morning while cutting a path through the tangled brash to the pond; by chance I cleared the thickets from around the open stump home. The mother cat, spitting a warning, her back arched, and her tail swollen, faced me without fear as her three tiny babies peered curiously from the hollow stump which her thin body blocked.

A pan of warm milk was left untouched and I found it frozen on the following day when I sought to coax the wild creature with some choice bits of fish which I spread on the icy ground near the crude habitation. But when the mother cat was finally convinced I had left the vicinity she ventured forth in search of food, and my opera glasses framed a picture near the stump: the three kittens all munching contentedly upon the larder their mother had disdained. That was the beginning of the disintegration of parental authority in that household. No matter how hard or how often the mother boxed the ears of her venturesome offspring, the longing for further adventures was in their souls and they began wandering out to the path leading to The Homestead whenever the mother would slip away on a hunting excursion.

One morning, when I opened the back door, there were the three kittens seated serenely on the mat awaiting my appearance. But in a flash Our Mary appeared in a frenzy of hostility, fur on end, teeth bared, and hissing loudly until I closed the door and she herded her rebellious offspring down the path to the stump. But the next morning, the three were again waiting on the mat and the pan of milk was lapped eagerly before the concerned mother herded them away.

It was Emmy, a therapist visiting from New York, who finally broke through the aloofness and fear of this mother cat. The soft voice of this gentle woman seemed to bring forth a forgotten trust in the heart of this lonely, outraged creature, and after some time she was eating civilized food along with her brood.

Our Mary, having deprived itself of practically all nourishment in her efforts to feed her hungry little ones, was in poor health when Emmy had intervened. The nutrients in the wheatgrass, mixed with the fish and the pure drinking water, brought forth changes. The whitish film over the cat's eyes began to slowly disappear; the circle on her forehead, between the eyes, which mange had robbed of hair, began to fur over, while the thin body filled out. But the real red-letter day of the reclamation of this wild creature was when, of her own accord, she climbed into the lap of the smiling Emmy and snuggled up under her arm.

It was shortly after her human friend left for home that Our Mary had a dangerous encounter. Nobody heard the battle, but the next morning when the door was opened, Our Mary, her white fur covered with drying blood, lay on the mat almost unable to move. Some large animal had apparently tangled with her. The left hind leg seemed out of place. It was hanging limply and the formerly sleek fur was slashed and rough. A cupful of freshly juiced wheatgrass was poured over the wounded animal and the injured leg was pushed back into place and bound with strong bandages. For the next week, the wounds were soaked periodically with wheatgrass juice, and when the bandages were removed at the end of two weeks, Our Mary seemed to be as good as new.

The veterinarians who watched the rejuvenation of this mal-treated animal through wheatgrass were surprised at the unex-pected healing power which seemed part of its natural qualities. The eye condition and the spreading mange had vanished com-pletely and never returned.

Our Mary taught us wonderful things, including how love and kindness can induce a wild creature to trust her former ene-mies. We human beings can learn much from such experiences.

## HONEYSUCKLE

I met Honeysuckle in a pet shop in Boston. I did not intend to acquire the little animal but while waiting for the clerk to find parakeet seed, I became involved in a distressing situation that ended only when Honeysuckle, tucked into a large carton, was placed on the back seat of my car. This tiny creature was a kin-kajou, the size of a half-grown cat, but it had demonstrated that it possessed the strength of a giant as it resisted the efforts of the proprietor and refused to return to the cage from which it had escaped. The elderly keeper of this miscellaneous commercial zoo was the victim of arthritis. He carried a heavy cane with which he began to beat the defiant little battier in a savage manner. It was at this juncture that I intervened. A bargain was soon consummated which made us both happy—he to get rid of "this pest," and I to add to my household another semi-wild animal on which could be tested the efficacy of the wheatgrass juice.

When I got Honeysuckle to my office, I began to look through my books in an effort to learn more about this new member of my family. I learned that the long, sharp teeth which had proved so devastating to the gloved hands of the pet shop owner indicated that my acquisition was a meat eater which dwelt among the tree-tops in the tropics, preying generally on birds and lizards. However, a footnote added, ripe fruit and honey were a regular part of its menu.

With this data, I cautiously began some experiments. It was necessary to proceed slowly because although the books stated the kinkajou was gentle and affectionate, the harsh treatment Honeysuckle had received during her short life had changed her into a mean-tempered beast who required careful handling. But it was a challenge. Could this little demon be remolded into a good-natured, playful creature in the same manner that Emmy had transformed Our Mary? During this attempt at domesticating Honeysuckle I felt that I might learn something of benefit to human beings.

First I tried ordinary honey as food. The little animal took a few licks with its long tongue and turned away. I inspected the label on the jar and found that the product had been heat-treated. So, I purchased some honey in the comb in a health food store, and Honeysuckle found this acceptable.

Since my new pet was a carnivore, I tried pieces of uncooked beef, lamb, and chicken. All were passed aside in favor of fresh fruit. Knowing her preference for fruit, I tried an experiment using frozen juice, which I placed in a saucer after diluting it according to directions. Honeysuckle merely sniffed and left it untouched.

Then I squeezed a little fresh orange juice into another saucer and the little creature lapped it up promptly.

This native of Mexico, Central America, and Northern South America was an enchanting addition to our household. She resembled a raccoon, with strong, wiry legs and miniature hands and long, heavy claw-like fingernails. When hungry she sat on her haunches, lifted the food in her fingers, peeled the skins from the fruit and fed daintily. Full grown, she was about the size of an ordinary cat, but with a longer and prehensile tail, which when anchored about something firm was difficult to dislodge.

Our visitor from the tropics gave ample warning before biting. Her loud and long hiss resembled that of an angry goose. Though my white cat Peter was naturally curious about this new addition to the family, he was not inclined to venture close to her.

After experiments with the feeding of Honeysuckle along the lines suggested by the officials of the local zoo, I began to add wisps of wheatgrass to her drinking water and to massage the bare spot on her forehead with freshly ground pulp. The result was gratifying. Before long the mood of the animal changed for the better and the area above the pointed nose began to fill in and blend with the surrounding yellowish-brown fur.

The process of domestication was slow, but eventually memories of cruel treatment were no longer present. Honeysuckle ate food from my plate and often traveled with me, her arms curled around my neck. What I learned from the little creature has been worth a thousand times the trouble she may have caused. In common with practically all animals, Honeysuckle ate only fresh, raw food.

Her refusal to eat meat puzzled me. Was it because the meat I could obtain was not as fresh as the birds and lizards caught alive and consumed immediately? Is it possible that something besides flavor, color, texture, and fragrance, something indispensable to health, is lost when foods are picked green, stored for a long time, frozen, canned, etc? Do wild animals, or those who are tamed later in life, know instinctively what is suitable food?

## OBSTINATE GUEST

In the winter of 1962 a short note arrived from a good friend in New York City, to the effect that his personal physician had suggested a short stay in the hospital to analyze the complaint for which he had consulted his doctors—a stoppage of his bowels. He had requested a consultation with two other doctors before agreeing to enter the hospital. The note explained, "... I am going there this afternoon where I expect to stay as few days as possible and where I'll prove to be a rather obstinate guest."

When I arrived at the office Monday morning, I found the telephone bell ringing. My good New York friend was on the wire, telling me he had returned from the hospital late the previous night and had been calling me regularly, every fifteen minutes, since five in the morning. His explanation was short: an X-ray of the bowel had revealed a growth the size of an apple pressing against the colon. The doctors had recommended an operation. He refused and asked for his clothing. They warned him of the danger if this condition continued for five or six more days, in addition to the several days already past. He told them he would give the first four of those five days to a test of the wheatgrass juice and that they would hear from him on the fifth day if the test failed. He asked for fresh wheatgrass that very afternoon, even if it were necessary to bribe a porter on a New York-bound train.

He got the first wheatgrass late that afternoon, and three days later I received a note that things had moved smoothly and the danger was seemingly over. His doctors were both relieved and puzzled.

For nearly a month, three drinks of the wheatgrass juice went into my friend's digestive system. Then I received a telephone call from him to the effect that he had promised his doctor that he would have another X-ray of the growth if he were still alive at the end of four weeks.

I made arrangements at once for an examination and X-rays at the medical clinic in Cambridge, where we occasionally refer our visitors at The Homestead. The following morning, my friend and his wife arrived.

Three days later the report of the clinic stated that there was a small growth on the side of the colon, about the size of a small hazel nut. An immediate operation was not advised under the circumstances.

That was many months ago and there is no indication of a return of the blockage of the bowel, so all thoughts of an operation were abandoned.

Can a growth of unknown origin in the interior of the body, where malignancy has not been determined, but which interferes with digestive processes by blocking the colon, be rendered harmless by anything but surgery? I make no assertion, but simply present the facts and let them speak for themselves.

## TURNABOUT

The following summer a couple from Arizona arrived at The Homestead. The woman suffered from chronic sores on the inner side of her plump legs, and had been informed that skin grafting was painful and dangerous, although her only solution. She persuaded her husband to drive her to Massachusetts to see what might be accomplished with the wheatgrass therapy.

For years she had been an invalid, lying in bed all day watching television and reading paper-back novels, while her husband went to work and did the housework. She had even managed to see that he carried into the car a television set that she might be amused during the long miles of travel. Frankly, I was shocked at their appearance. The woman was blond, well-built, plump, and except for the painful leg sores, a picture of health, stretched out at ease in the hinged front car seat. The husband was a man over sixty who was frail, nervous, and as solicitous of his wife's comfort as the proverbial mother hen with the single chick.

It was easy to see that every whim of this woman was a command to him. When he finally got her settled in a room on the second floor and came downstairs for a bite to eat, she called to him over the banister to "come up here" so that he could sit beside her while she watched her favorite television program. Halfway up the stairs, he stopped to get his breath.

In the two days which followed, I saw that the wrong person was stretched out on the comfortable couch on the floor above. That evening I had a good friend, a medical doctor, come in. Without disclosing his identity, I let him examine the husband in a routine manner. His report made the resolution I had half-decided upon take definite form.

So next morning, when the husband was trudging a mile to the village for some strawberries that "she is crazy about," I mounted the stairs and told the lady some facts about her husband, including that there was a possibility that he might "leave" her at almost any time.

The results were electrical. When the panting husband got back with the strawberries he was met downstairs at the door by his fully-dressed wife, her hair combed and a smile of welcome on her face. And for the ensuing twenty minutes, the bewildered man let himself be pushed out into the open air for a sunbath, a pillow plumped under his thin shoulders. During that short interval he probably received more personal attention from his "partner" than had been his lot during the entire trip from Arizona.

When his wife finally retired upstairs "to rest," clutching her strawberries, the man sat in a sort of unbelieving stupor, gazing at the flower garden by the porch, and shaking his head slowly back and forth in puzzled ecstasy. Later, I explained what I had done, and cautioned him to "take it easy."

The wife took her wheatgrass juice three times a day, "so my good husband will relish his," as she put it. Several improvements resulted. The sarcastic tone left her voice, she began to smile instead of frown, and the sores on her legs healed rapidly. When the couple left three weeks later, she wept on my shoulder, calling me the savior of her home. They vanished down the road, both waving goodbye from the car.

And then—silence. Months passed and not a word of any kind was received from them. But a friend of the husband, living in a nearby trailer, wrote me that the couple was continuing the use of wheatgrass and living food and the woman was up and about for the first time in years.

But beyond that brief statement—more silence. We do not expect appreciation, but I do regret that we have no letters from either the husband or wife telling of the improvement both had experienced through the wheatgrass regimen. Other couples might be helped to understand that many times, the partner who is seemingly an invalid is, in fact, the healthier of the two, and the uncomplaining one who is seeking to carry on may actually be very close to collapse.

## AN "IMPOSSIBLE" WOMAN

A social worker described this unfortunate woman as impossible: "She will not help herself, and while something ought to be done for her, whoever attempts it will find it a thankless job."

With that introduction I made my way into the shabby house and up the stairs where I knocked on the door of this invalid. Although the hour was past noon, and I had completed the regular daily chore of bringing fresh wheatgrass juice to a dozen individuals, the weak voice which greeted me formed the words: "Go away, I am in bed. Come back later."

I replied that lack of time would prevent me, that I had been sent to help her and if she did not choose to talk now, the opportunity would not come again. Evidently this aroused her curiosity, for I heard her shambling across the room; she unbolted and opened the door. The haggard face of a prematurely old woman of about thirty-five, with uncombed hair, greeted me. Without an invitation, I found a chair while she slowly climbed into bed, moaning. It was then I noted a tired-looking collie dog tied to a table leg and I could not help wondering how this little animal existed in such surroundings.

Accustomed as I was to the disheveled, hopeless human beings who were receiving the daily wheatgrass beverage, I was nevertheless shocked by this disintegrating wreck of a young body, listless and without the vestige of a desire to help herself. For weeks she had been practically bed-ridden, with neighbors walking the dog at uncertain times. On the nearby table I saw the array of bottles of medicine, which according to the report kept "the poor thing in an almost continuous stupor." I realized that convincing this semi-invalid to take the wheatgrass juice each day would be a most difficult task. But I wanted to see for myself what it might be able to accomplish for this individual, whose illness had been diagnosed as multiple sclerosis.

So I stayed with her for a while, took the dog out for a walk, and was back the next day with a sample drink. She took it reluctantly, I believe just to please me, because her wry face indicated her dislike for the flavor.

That was the beginning. Within two weeks the sufferer was out of bed, usually waiting beside her door in the upper hall when I arrived. Her smile of greeting paid me for everything. The change was really amazing. Within a month the pajamas had been discarded and the usually cluttered room was neater than it had been in a long, long time. I celebrated with her on the morning she greeted me with, "And I took Pal out for a walk yesterday afternoon myself."

In two months she was at the beauty parlor, her first visit there in several years. The old lethargy was gone, her eyes were bright, and the lines in her face had softened. As she put on the new dress her sister had sent she was really an attractive woman.

Incredible as it may seem, within six months she was married. Can you wonder that I look upon this God-sent wheat-grass juice and new diet as something precious?

Since the above situation, which ended so well, I have had many letters from others with this dread affliction and all seemed to have benefited by using the simple diet and the regular wheat-grass juice.

However, the real, convincing proof for all multiple sclerosis victims is to use this approach under their doctor's supervision. As we know, nerve tissue cannot regenerate itself. It is significant, though, that there are medically verified cases of remission, some of years' standing.

## MY FRIEND JOHN, A FORMER DIABETIC

According to *Today's Health Guide*, published in 1968 by the American Medical Association, diabetes is a disorder in which the body fails to make proper use of sugar. The sugar accumulates in the blood and often passes into the urine, which is discharged in excessive quantities. Diabetes is believed to be the result of the failure of the pancreas gland to produce enough insulin regularly to keep the sugar level of the blood down to the point scientists have determined is normal. There seems to be no medicine which will permanently and completely cure the disease, but relief is afforded and the sugar content of the blood is decreased when insulin, taken from the pancreas of a cow or pig, is injected directly into the bloodstream at regular intervals. Insulin therapy must often be continued for the lifetime of the diabetic. Oral or tablet treatment is limited to milder cases in older people. Diabetes may be controlled by diet alone in at least half of the patients who develop the disease after the age of thirty, says the same Guide, as in some cases the disease improves with treatment.

Recently, however, a group of researchers kept the pancreas of a deceased diabetic alive outside the body for more than six hours. They found that it would produce all the insulin necessary to keep the sugar in the blood at a safe level. It appears that this ample insulin is unused in the diabetic because of an interference somewhere, possibly a stoppage of the two tiny tubes that are supposed to carry the insulin into the top of the small intestine. It may be that this blockage prevents the insulin from getting into the blood and it is thrown out of the body as waste. This permits the sugar level of the blood to rise, resulting in diabetes. The researchers in this field are now looking for a drug which will correct this blockage and permit the insulin to flow normally. A score of years may elapse before this development is brought about so that diabetics can make use of it.

In the meantime, we have found that the diabetic who regularly takes wheatgrass juice and follows the simple raw food diet is able to cut down on the dose of insulin. One diabetic under the supervision of medical doctors in a large Massachusetts hospital was able to cut down his insulin intake in one week using wheat-grass juice.

Here is the history of a good friend, let me call him "John," who came to The Homestead in 1962. According to the record, his health failed in 1957 and a period at a Midwestern hospital disclosed diabetes. When he was discharged, at the end of six days of testing, he carried with him a hypodermic needle and the information that it was likely that he must inject insulin into his body each day. For the next five years he followed the injection routine stolidly, but in 1962 his condition worsened. The future seemed black indeed.

He became interested in natural methods for achieving health. About April of that year a sheet showing what the simple diet and the wheatgrass juice was doing for others, came into his hands. The regimen seemed logical to him as his own physical condition had become noticeably better when he had increased his use of organically grown vegetables and fruits. He decided to try wheat-grass and planted a large area of wheat seed. Within seven days he had ample wheatgrass for his purpose. Then came the test. He stopped his insulin and drank two large tumblers of wheatgrass juice with water, and he did this each day for six weeks. His new vigor and increasing optimism sent him hurrying to his regular physician at the end of twenty-one days. His doctor could find no trace of diabetes. But of course, John and the physician could not be sure. So for the next month and a half weekly tests were made which disclosed the sugar content of his blood to be normal, indicating that he was receiving all the insulin from his pancreas that his body required. In the several months John stayed at The Homestead, his tests for diabetes were negative. And following his departure, the same condition held true.

It is my hope that other sufferers with diabetes, who have grown tired of the seemingly endless taking of insulin—will decide to make the wheatgrass test on their own bodies, under their physician's supervision, of course. It is important to remember that you will need to take the wheatgrass juice regularly and adopt the living foods diet permanently.

Sufferers with kidney troubles who have tried the diet and the wheatgrass juice also find it beneficial. Malfunctioning kidneys are an extremely serious problem. It may be that something has clogged the tiny fiber-like tubes of the sensitive organs and only Nature, supplied with the nutrients she requires to "swab out" the thousands of minute passages, can once again free the intricate mechanism so it may run properly. The diet and the wheatgrass juice have proved to be successful cleansers of the kidneys.

## OUR INDISPENSABLE DOCTORS

My grandmother, who exerted such a positive influence over me in my early years, taught me that every reasonable prayer would be answered. As I grew older, I seemed to find her advice correct, yet when I came to this country and began to study for the ministry, I discovered that many problems could not be solved entirely through prayer. It took me years of pain and misery before I was convinced that this was so.

The enlightenment began when I was feeding my chickens one winter's morning in 1960 and made too great an effort to break loose a pail frozen to the snow-covered earth. A great pain suddenly swept through my groin and I doubled up on the ground, hardly able to breathe. Some way I got into the house where I spent hours of agony on my couch. From that moment I was more or less an invalid. I did not dare tell my household of my trouble, as illness of any kind was unheard of among us. It was not until a year later that the difficulty was diagnosed as a hernia.

I knew God could heal this affliction and I began to pray faithfully for such relief. I learned also that such healings had been brought about without hospital and surgical care but were accomplished by something my work would not permit—spending months in bed. Of course, I was not discouraged at the outlook because my grandmother had assured me that spiritual healing was available always to the dedicated, and I felt my faith was sufficient.

One of the reasons I joined the religious school in the Midwest, where I studied during the autumn, was to bring about this healing within my body. Following the instructions of my teachers I would sit for hours, unmoving, praying for the help I knew God could give.

The months slipped into years and my condition seemed to be getting worse, rather than better. Finally, I could hardly move about, could not straighten my body and was in constant agony.

Then one morning I had a great awakening, when I suddenly realized that I was using my own conviction as to how this problem should be met, instead of asking God what I should do. It came as a sort of inspiration, a brilliant flash that suddenly lighted up my entire being. I returned to my room, closed the door and prayed, not for healing, not for anything but wisdom, to be shown what I should do.

In this instance the answer was forthcoming in short minutes. Almost in a dream I saw myself slip back into those days of my childhood, stretched underneath that old oak tree by the spring as my herd of goats and sheep, under the watchful eye of my lead dog, Star, munched the deep green grass by the willows. Once more I saw the mother squirrel, Mrs. Chatter, her injured leg encased in clay, dragging herself from the tall reeds by the stream. And just beside her, in the deep swamp, was Whitey, my grandmother's little dog, his leg deep in the black mud, standing patiently as the poison of a snake bite were somehow neutralized by the soft muck. Then I was back in the present and once more heard the chattering of the blackbirds in the hollow behind the garage. But in that momentary flashback, the wisdom I prayed for was manifested.

Now I understood. God, with His limitless power, could have healed these little animals of my childhood days. But through the God-guided instinct of each, the need for health became overpowering and thus the healing aid of the clay and the mud was sought, making it possible for God to bless the final results with renewed health. I realized why my prayers were unanswered. Through the exercise of my free will I had allowed my prejudices against the use of outside aid to blind me to the realities of everyday life and had pushed aside the advice of friends who were only seeking my welfare. At long last I began to comprehend fully that since I could not confine my body to bed for several months, I must seek the outside help available and become once again fit to work at full capacity.

As the force of my folly burst upon me, I sat there on the couch with my mind flitting back and forth between my childhood experiences and the facts of everyday life, and there took shape within my being a simple instruction: "Have an operation."

The impact stunned me. My relatives had suggested this method of relief, as had my good friend Dr. Alonzo J. Shadman. But I had been so sure that physical help was unnecessary, that spiritual help was so certain, that I had not listened to their entreaties. But now I was face to face with reality, made my way downstairs, called Dr. Shadman on the telephone and asked him to recommend a surgeon. "That is sensible, Ann," he said. "If you could remain in bed for months the hernia might heal itself, I have heard of such cases. But you are too active. It simply could not work out. I shall call you back when I have made arrangements."

Two hours later they had been made and the next morning I was in the operating room. The physician who was preparing me for the operation gave me spinal anesthesia. I did not feel the knife, but when out from under the effect of the drug, after the operation, I found myself in considerable pain. The orders were for me to have food, after some time. But I felt from the experiences I had had with my grandmother in helping the sick that no food should be taken. I had seen her treat many wounds. In every instance, the sufferer, no matter how thin, would be given nothing but warm water and juices.

The attending physician came in to request that I follow the routine of the hospital, but I preferred to have no injections and take no sedatives despite the pains which kept me in bed for six days. The result was gratifying. The nurses were surprised at the quick healing of the cut, where no sign of the operation was visible without a close inspection. At the end of seven days, I left the hospital happy at no longer having to endure the pain of an untreated hernia.

But the experience was valuable to me. It demonstrated that while faith healing might be a most essential part of one's religious belief, there were instances where medical help must be sought. When there are broken bones, it is far better to allow an expert to re-set them than for the sufferer to try to accomplish this purpose through prayer. Where there is a cut artery or a severed vein, skilled assistance is required. I could enumerate scores of instances where a common-sense procedure should take precedence over religious means. The skill of a well-trained doctor can often make the difference between life and death, between a sound body and a crippled one, between comfort and discomfort.

## ELIMINATION OF A DEATH TRAP

I would be remiss, indeed, if I did not put into the record that I believe this country—this "fabulous land" as the folks in our European village used to call it—is the most liveable spot on earth. I am glad I was not born here because if I were I could not appreciate the opportunity spreading before everyone. It requires knowing from hard experience what other countries are like before you can see what this nation "under God" actually means to every man, woman, and child. Every man, woman, and child should be healthy.

That is why I am a citizen. That is why I vote. That is why I expect to remain here as long as possible on His business, helping anyone who is interested to learn how to aid Mother Nature in her repair work by supplying their "temples" with the most suitable type of nourishment.

Of course, even here everything is not perfect. Neither was the Garden of Eden. But in the "land of the free" improvement is always possible with His help, always at the fingertips of the majority of its inhabitants who have only to go to the polls. In no other country is that fact as true as it is here. If we are willing to work for what we want we can get it and the small voice is often heard despite the shouts of those who try to silence it.

I faced a difficult political situation recently. It centered about a "death trap" close to my office here in Boston. A stone abutment, bordering the opening where the trolley cars emerged from underground, constituted the menace. Through an unfortunate widening of the street at this point, any motorist unfamiliar with the locality who attempted to pass the car ahead under conditions that ordinarily would have been safe, was suddenly confronted with a dead end.

Four persons had died at that spot in as many years. At ordinary speed, in the semi-darkness, they had crashed into this stone wall. Merchants of the neighborhood had tried vainly to induce the authorities to put a blinking yellow light on that abutment. Their efforts had met the usual political promises coupled with the customary notation that the matter was under consideration. But the weeks of delay rolled into months and the months settled down into years.

It was the last victim that roused me to action. He had died in early April, crushed under his automobile engine. When I viewed the spot the next day, a hollow in the pavement was still filled with the blood which had dripped from his shattered body. I left the scene with the determination to do something to rectify this monstrous situation. I felt that it was my responsibility. Letters were sent to public officials, but brought only the usual "promises." Finally, having gathered a sheaf full of such assurances of "immediate action," I wrote a summary of them to the mayor and told him I would be forced to publish the whole disgraceful correspondence unless these assurances were immediately implemented. That did it. A letter came from the Traffic Commissioner, stating that a blinker would be installed on the spot without delay and that a contract had already been signed with the local Edison Company guaranteeing its maintenance. And so, shortly thereafter (the negotiations had consumed over four months) the beacon, blinking its yellow warning, appeared on that dangerous abutment.

I feel that this light, as it winks safety with every flash, vividly demonstrates what the conscientious efforts of any one single individual, without appreciable backing, may accomplish despite the predictions of some. Every person must take such actions.

## WHEATGRASS THERAPY SPANS THE WORLD

The people around us have an enormous influence in the shaping of our lives and our world. For me, the most compelling personality I ever met was my grandmother. A person with extraordinary energy and with complete devotion to the code of decency and humanity, she did more to influence my later years than all the hardships, happiness, hopes, and wonders which unfolded as time went on. It was the morning after my horrible experience in the quicksands of the swamp that she led me out into the sunshine and we sat beside the well curb. For some moments she was silent, clasping me tightly in her arms. Then she spoke along these lines.

"When I heard the alarmed barks of Star coming from the swamp, Annetta, I knew something terrible was wrong. But, actually, I felt no real concern about your safety. From the moment I rescued you from your father I have had a God-inspired certainty that you were destined to be a means whereby humanity would be bettered, physically and spiritually. You have seen distressing times in our house and have witnessed the passing of good folks and bad. Through it all you have been a great help to me as you will be a help to others in the future. But I want you to know in your deepest being that you are destined for an important part in God's plan. We all have our allotted tasks. How yours will come about I do not know. But it will come, never fear, and you must prepare for that moment and be ready to take your place as a part of His wondrous pattern."

I will never forget that little talk. It is engraved upon my soul. With the discovery of the health-promoting wheat-grass therapy, I realized that my kindly, loving grandmother had indeed seen into the future, and that the possibility of aiding suffering humanity everywhere is a demonstrated fact. Once more I repeat—she was a great healer, one of the greatest, I am sure, who ever lived.

Fortunately, I have been able to present the elements of the wheatgrass therapy so that publishers of various periodicals throughout the country have grasped much of the significance of what I have sought to accomplish and during the many years since the discovery of the benefits of wheat-grass, comprehensive articles on living food and sprouts have appeared regularly.

In foreign countries, the information has been given to those who need it by many journals. One result is I have received thousands of letters. A comment from a sincere man in London might bear repeating here. He wrote me a lengthy letter and among other things he had this to say:

"Why should the revelation which led you to this miraculous wheatgrass have been given to you? What have you done to deserve this sincere trust of the Almighty that you would handle the information wisely and selflessly? I am as interested in health as you. My whole life has been devoted to aiding others less fortunate than myself. Why should you have been favored rather than me?"

I think, in this connection, of the moving poem by John Milton, "On His Blindness," the last line of which reads, "They also serve who only stand and wait." And is it not true that we all contribute in our own way, and that we are all equally important? But each of us are given tasks which we are ready to undertake.

The most gratifying fact of all, to me, is that in England, Australia, New Zealand, France, South Africa, Syria, India, West Germany, Spain, Singapore, Austria, Pakistan, and many places in South America the wheatgrass has been tested in a most practical way—by the ailing—and in every instance of which I have knowledge those tests have brought most satisfactory results.

# CHAPTER FIVE

# The Nucleus is Formed

## MARGARET DRUMHELLER'S VISIT

It was the summer of 1962, and the organic gardens at The Homestead, which grew larger and more bountiful each year, were in full bloom. The fertile black soil, enriched by the use of compost, yielded the most nutritious and tasty vegetables, fruits, and edible weeds. Needless to say I was kept busy during those long warm days at The Homestead. There were my usual letters and articles to write, as well as gardening, shopping, and caring for the small but growing number of guests staying with me.

One very humid afternoon during the dog days of July, I received a phone call from my friend Beverly, who was then living in New York. She was to be in Boston in a couple of days and wanted to visit The Homestead with a friend of hers from Boston named Margaret. I invited them to lunch, and eagerly awaited their visit.

When Beverly and Margaret arrived that afternoon I was somewhat out of sorts, having undertaken the Herculean task of cleaning the house and weeding most of the garden before preparing lunch for a dozen people. After a few deep breaths I walked to the driveway to greet them.

Margaret was a good-looking woman of medium height and build, with a rather distinctive air about her. Her dress and posture gave an impression of culture and refinement. Indeed, she was well-read in many fields, including philosophy, religion, literature, and current events, and had traveled extensively for many years of her life. Our conversation that day during lunch renewed me like the first green grass of spring. Margaret had a thousand questions about my work which I did my best to answer. And I in turn inquired about her adventures and philosophy of life.

It was getting late, and I was thinking about starting dinner, when Margaret broke in. "Ann," she said, "If you really want to help people to become well again, why not come to Boston where many more people in need of your knowledge can more easily reach you?" I explained that I had often thought of returning to Boston to live and further expand my work. But I had little money, and The Homestead could not function without me. "Too bad," Margaret said, "I own a building on Exeter St. in Boston's Back Bay, and I have extra space for rent. Why not take it," she said, "You can pay the rent with the money you make from teaching and helping others."

It seemed once again as if fate had intervened in my life. Here was this wonderful woman offering me a chance to bring my work to a new level—to reach out to a greater number of people and to form an organization (with her help) in the city. Margaret would not take "no" for an answer, and so I agreed to visit her in the city to look at the rooms and discuss possible arrangements with her at that time.

## A NEW HOME IN BOSTON

Though the next few days were as demanding as always, I could think of little else except my next visit with Margaret. I had busily thought through all of the wonderful possibilities moving my work to the city would offer. It would allow me to meet many more of the people I had corresponded with over the years through the *Natural Health Guardian* magazine. Most of all, it would place me closer to the various government and private institutions with which I had hoped to contact and work. This was truly an exciting week. Margaret's building was an impressive five-story brick structure located at the corner of Exeter Street and Commonwealth Avenue. It overlooked the tree-lined park which runs into the Boston Public Gardens—a beautiful spot indeed.

When Margaret greeted me at the front door I could hardly conceal my excitement. She invited me in and took me on a short tour of the building. The first floor was split into three large rooms which were occupied by a travel agency. The walls, staircase, and moulding were adorned with hand-carved hardwood designs and figures. The high ceilings and attention to detail reflected an earlier era of prosperity and charm.

The second, third, and fourth floors were a combination of separate rooms and apartments. Margaret brought me to see the two large rooms on the second floor which were to be my new home and office in Boston. It was with suppressed excitement that I viewed these spacious quarters. Now, truly, I could help to heal and minister to the large number of sufferers, whose ill health deprived them of all the joys of life, by taking them into my care and seeing that they benefited from the simple living foods diet and wheatgrass juice therapy. It wasn't without a struggle, though, that Margaret prevailed upon me to take these rooms. They were perfect, but I had no funds with which to pay rent and I didn't really expect to have a tremendous cash flow while I sought to establish a new base. I later learned that this caring and intelligent woman had an abiding personal interest in my endeavor. She hoped to share in the excitement and learning that accompanied my new venture.

A short time later I moved in. Beds were placed in both rooms. In one of the rooms I cared for my new city guests, mostly seriously ill and older people. The other room became my bedroom, living room, and office. Later I occupied a third room, which I also set up to house guests. In this way I began the building of what was to become the Hippocrates Health Institute.

## THE HIPPOCRATES HEALTH INSTITUTE

In contrast to the past few years, which had been ones of strengthening my body and solidifying my ideas on diet, health, and spiritual development, the next several years were to be devoted to establishing the Institute. A lawyer was contacted, and applications were filled out requesting non-profit, educational, and charitable legal status for the organization.

In time, I came to occupy several rooms in Margaret's building and was able to pay her a fair rent in exchange. In addition, Margaret volunteered to become my bookkeeper, making deposits for me and otherwise handling the finances. Then one day she brought me devastating news: for financial and personal reasons, she was forced to sell the building! She had a buyer in mind, and if I were to continue to build on my promising beginnings on Exeter Street, I had but a few days to come up with money I did not have to buy the building.

I convinced Margaret to accompany me to the bank where her original mortgage was drawn. Initially I got nowhere with the loan officer, who told me it was highly irregular for them to tend money of the quantity I needed without a sizable down-payment on my part. It was Margaret who once again saved the day. Somehow she convinced the bank to refinance the building in my name, with a scant two-hundred-dollar deposit.

With a building and legal status for the organization, the Hippocrates Health Institute was born, despite my limited cash flow and the as yet somewhat marginal support for my work. Perhaps more than anything else, my faith in the importance of my work, and the confidence of knowing that whatever I needed to continue would be provided, gave me the strength to endure those hard times.

My early years had been filled with struggle and toil, yet I now worked longer and harder than ever before. At times I felt exhausted, but I was never discouraged for long because every day I saw in the bright eyes and smiling faces of my guests who had arrived in weak and despairing condition, the importance of my task. I could not let these people down. By sheer determination I was able to make ends meet. Little did I know that a new era for my work was soon to blossom forth. With the help of various publications I was involved in, including books and pamphlets, and by word of mouth, people began hearing about and visiting the Institute. To my great surprise, many of them were young and quite idealistic. They had plenty of energy and proved to be of tremendous help in accomplishing the every day chores of growing and preparing the wheatgrass, sprouts, and greens for the guests, cleaning the house, answering the phones, typing, and helping those guests who were weakened by the ravages of disease.

## THE PRINCIPLES OF HEALTH

I would like to end this book with a few words about my philosophy: health is what one makes of it. It requires a mature attitude and self-discipline to rebuild failing health. Beyond these requirements a simple and energetic diet, exercise, and a healthy outlook are vital. Ideally, all of us would see the common sense in these ideas and work to prevent any imbalances before they occur. By and large, however, the kind of prevention being practiced today is of a secondary nature. That is, "I have had a heart attack—please keep me from having another," or "I have cancer—please keep it from spreading."

The best prevention, either primary or secondary, is the strengthening and "sensitizing" of the body. In this "sensitizing" process, the individual gains an increased awareness of his body, and its reactions to his lifestyle. The body is continually providing us with all sorts of important messages that are the key to survival, either in the form of energy and vitality (the result of good health practices), or pain and illness (the result of disharmony). The idea behind the Hippocrates program is to establish harmony and vitality in the body through changes in the individual's day-today lifestyle, particularly with respect to diet. For if a way of living does not keep the body balanced and healthy, it is not in harmony with the goals and purposes of our lives.

Simple, uncooked foods such as fresh vegetables, greens, fruits, sprouted seeds, grains, beans, and nuts, along with pure liquids such as fresh vegetable juices, fruit juices, and "green drinks" made from a variety of sprouts, greens, and vegetables, are nutritious yet light on digestion.

In my years of working with this simple diet, I have observed that after following such a diet for a number of weeks, many people notice the disappearance of nagging problems they had lived with for months or years. Blocked sinuses open up, sleep is deeper and more restful, aches and pains are relieved, excess weight is quickly shed, the eyes become brighter, and facial stress disappears.

After a few months on the diet, the development of an entirely new attitude is not uncommon—one that reflects self-confidence in matters of health, rather than submission and dependence on others. In fact, if my years of training and experience in working with thousands of people have proven one thing, it is that we can learn to control our level of health and the course of our lives if we choose. The building up of this degree of self-reliance may take some time, but it is well worth the effort and the wait. I have explored my ideas on diet and health more fully in The Hippocrates Diet and Health Program, published by Avery Publishing Group.

In this fast-paced world it is too frequently the case that people accept what society, family members, and the authorities whom nobody ever seems to question, believe regarding how to live their lives. And yet, the happiest people I know have been those who have accepted the primary responsibility for their own spiritual and physical well-being—those who have inner strength, courage, determination, common sense, and faith in the process of creating more balanced and satisfying lives for themselves.

# So...
# WHY
# SUFFER?

Join us for an educational ten-day Living Foods Lifestyle® reTREAT at the original Ann Wigmore Foundation®! *Come live and learn the original Dr. Ann program.*

**Allow your healing and nurturing to begin!**
Come vacation, live with us and learn, and return to a state of healing balance.

**For more information,**
contact the
Ann Wigmore Foundation®
by calling
505-552-0595 or
visit us online:
annwigmore.com
wigmore.org
livingfoodsgardenvillage.com

**Other books by Dr. Ann Wigmore**

*The Miracles of Wheatgrass*

*Rebuild your Health*

*Recipes for Longer Life*

*The Alchemy of Change*

*You Are the Light of the World*

*Be Your Own Doctor*

*From Fat to Fit*

*Why You Do Not Need to Grow Old*

*Recipes for Total Health and Youth*

and many more!

# Book Publishing Co.

*books that educate, inspire, and empower*

To find your favorite vegetarian and soyfood products online, visit:
www.healthy-eating.com

Hippocrates LifeForce
*Brian R. Clement, PhD, NMD, LNC*
978-1-57067-249-1 $14.95

Becoming Raw
*Brenda Davis, RD, and*
*Vesanto Melina, MS, RD,*
*with Rynn Berry*
978-1-57067-238-5 $24.95

Food IS Medicine
*Brian R. Clement, PhD, NMD, LNC*
978-1-57067-274-3 $29.95

Raw Food Made Easy for
One or Two People
*Revised Edition*
*Jennifer Cornbleet*
978-1-57067-273-6 $19.95

Survival in the 21st Century
*Viktoras H. Kulvinskas, MS*
978-1-57067-247-7 $29.95

Purchase these health titles and cookbooks from your local bookstore or natural food store,
or you can buy them directly from:

Book Publishing Company • P.O. Box 99 • Summertown, TN 38483 • 1-800-695-2241

*Please include $3.95 per book for shipping and handling.*